Grieving The Loss Of A Loved One

H. Norman Wright
Author Of Helping Those In Grief

EasyRead Large

Copyright Page from the Original Book

Published by Regal
From Gospel Light
Ventura, California, U.S.A.
www.regalbooks.com
Printed in the U.S.A.

All Scripture quotations, unless otherwise indicated, are taken from the *Holy Bible, New International Version*®. Copyright © 1973, 1978, 1984 by International Bible Society. Used by permission of Zondervan Publishing House. All rights reserved.

Other versions used are
AMP—Scripture taken from the *Amplified® Bible*, Copyright © 1954, 1958, 1962, 1964, 1965, 1987 by The Lockman Foundation. Used by permission.
ESV—Scripture taken from the *English Standard Version*, Copyright © 2001. The *ESV* and *English Standard Version* are trademarks of Good News Publishers.
GNB—Scripture taken from the Good News Translation, Second Edition, Copyright 1992 by American Bible Society. Used by Permission.
KJV—*King James Version*. Authorized King James Version.
THE MESSAGE—Scripture taken from *THE MESSAGE*. Copyright © 1993, 1994, 1995, 1996, 2000, 2001, 2002. Used by permission of NavPress Publishing Group.
NASB—Scripture taken from the *New American Standard Bible*, © 1960, 1962, 1963, 1968, 1971, 1972, 1973, 1975, 1977, 1995 by The Lockman Foundation. Used by permission.
NCV—Scriptures quoted from *The Holy Bible, New Century Version,* copyright © 1987, 1988, 1991 by Word Publishing, Nashville, Tennessee. Used by permission.
NLT—Scripture quotations marked *NLT* are taken from the *Holy Bible, New Living Translation,* copyright © 1996, 2004, 2007 by Tyndale House Foundation. Used by permission of Tyndale House Publishers, Inc., Carol Stream, Illinois 60188. All rights reserved.
TLB—Scripture quotations marked (*TLB*) are taken from *The Living Bible,* copyright © 1971. Used by permission of Tyndale House Publishers, Inc., Wheaton, IL 60189. All rights reserved.

© 2013 H. Norman Wright
All rights reserved.

Library of Congress Cataloging-in-Publication Data
Wright, H. Norman.
Grieving the loss of a loved one / H. Norman Wright.
pages cm
Includes bibliographical references and index.
ISBN 978-0-8307-6638-3 (alk. paper)
1. Grief—Religious aspects—Christianity. 2. Bereavement—Religious aspects—Christianity. 3. Loss (Psychology)—Religious aspects—Christianity. I. Title.
BV4909.W75 2013
248.8'66—dc22
2013006135

Rights for publishing this book outside the U.S.A. or in non-English languages are administered by Gospel Light Worldwide, an international not-for-profit ministry. For additional information, please visit www.glww.org, email info@glww.org, or write to Gospel Light Worldwide, 1957 Eastman Avenue, Ventura, CA 93003, U.S.A.

To order copies of this book and other Regal products in bulk quantities, please contact us at 1-800-446-7735.

TABLE OF CONTENTS

Introduction	i
1: The World of Grief	1
2: The Loss of a Spouse	45
3: The Death of a Child	87
4: Helping Children in Grief	140
5: The Death of a Parent	176
6: Parent Loss—A Woman and Her Mother; A Man and His Father	201
7: The Loss of a Sibling	230
8: The Loss of a Friend	257
9: The Loss of a Pet	280
10: The Questions of Life	317
11: Helping Others	343
Endnotes	379
Additional Resources	397
Front Cover Flap	402
Back Cover Flap	404
Back Cover Material	405

Introduction

If you are reading this book, you have probably experienced a loss in your life. It could be one of the worst in your life—the death of a family member. Losses abound in life, but we would rather avoid them, especially the loss of a loved one.

When a member of your immediate family dies, you experience a painful transition from your familiar world. You are plunged into a new life that you don't like. This death can also end or threaten your plans for the future.

When you lose a family member, it's not only an individual loss. Yes, your life will be impacted, but so will the entire family's. What you knew as family is gone. All of you will have to discover how to function together in a new way. There is a shift in the balance of your family. Who is supposed to do what? Some roles are obvious and some are not.

Each member of your family will respond differently to the loss because of his or her own losses and relationship with the deceased. Everyone will struggle and make adjustments. What if someone wants to empty the house, but the others want it left intact with pictures up? What if someone wants the traditional holiday, but others want it changed? What if the inheritance doesn't seem fair to everyone?

The loss of any family member throws the entire family into crisis. To understand the enormous stress that a death inflicts on the family as a whole—and on each of its members—it is helpful to consider your family's functioning methods during routine times. To what degree do you believe your family was healthy? A healthy, unstressed family will operate under certain circumstances and systems. Each family member in the system is related by heredity and emotions to each of the others, and each member is crucial to the family's organization and balanced functioning powers. Your family unit provides protection and sustenance to you and to each person within the unit, and gives a sense of belonging and togetherness. Each of you has found his or her own identity within this unit but also has realized that each was a separate individual.

Any family death disrupts the delicate balance between the family togetherness and its members' individuality. Whoever has died held a specific role of importance to the family structure. Eventually, the remaining family members will assume these responsibilities. The surviving parent will take on those obligations that require an adult's experience. The children will fill in with those abilities that are in keeping with their ages and development. Until this occurs, though, the family's normal patterns of interacting are short-circuited. Before new and successful family patterns can be established, each family member must make significant adjustments. This includes not only your role as a family member but also your relationship to every family member. This is not a step easily taken in the midst of suffering.

Before the construction of new family roles can begin, each person needs time and space to absorb the loss in his or her own way. All members must maintain the ability to disengage from the unit when necessary. But disengagement can be carried too far.

How do you see others grieving as well as changing their roles? What difficulties do you anticipate? What do you need from each other? What do all the other family members need from you?

Some deaths are considered natural and timely. They're expected, especially at a certain age and with accompanying physical problems. But many others are not expected.

Death comes in many forms, bringing with it varying degrees of pain, sorrow and grief. When it comes, it disrupts your life story. It is a time when you are vulnerable in several areas.

You are vulnerable in your connections with those who die. Objects, things, places, events and other people are always there to remind you of your loss. Personal items, where your loved one lived, the places your loved one frequented, their special days and events—all are reminders that impact you.

You're also vulnerable to the loss of stability. Your daily routines and life patterns have been disrupted. The more you were involved in the everyday life of the deceased loved one, the greater your adjustment to the loss. You see yourself no longer as a complete person now that your loved one is gone. It's difficult to go on with life *without,* and you may feel incomplete in your present life story. It's difficult to see the future as you once did. Many say they feel fragmented. Perhaps you do as well.

You may have unfinished business—plans and dreams for the future; conversations you meant to have or needed to have; the cessation of what you expected to take place in the next five years; not being able to share yourself with the person, or not being able to say "Goodbye" or "I love you" or "Please forgive me" or "I forgive you." If the death was a child, you're denied the opportunity to nurture and teach and watch the child grow up.

You may experience the continuing effect of a painful relationship. It's difficult to cope with loss when there were strong negative feelings complicating your grief. You may experience guilt or anger over your feelings toward the person. Perhaps you were ministered to or, just the opposite, traumatized by the deceased, or perhaps it was the other way around. Possibly you feel responsible for the death or for failing to meet the person's needs.

You may experience "disenfranchised" grieving. The support of others at this time is vital, but for various reasons, others may not recognize or validate your grief. They may not see the loss as that significant and thus may not give the comfort and support you need, or they may make inappropriate comments. This can be devastating and can intensify your grief as well as your feelings of abandonment and alienation.

You may feel vulnerable because of the circumstances surrounding the death. Sudden, unexpected and traumatic death can overwhelm as well as delay acceptance of the reality of what has occurred. If you were the caregiver for months or years, your exhaustion can make it difficult to process grief.

You may experience limits in your coping ability. Even if you have good coping abilities, you may discover that what worked for you before doesn't work at this time. The onslaught of intense and overwhelming emotions creates a paralysis. Weak areas that were well hidden before will emerge, and unresolved issues and losses from the past will resurface. Personal and relational dysfunctions may intensify. To add to all of these issues is the problem of our culture's inability to face death and the grieving process. Having to learn about the process of grief while experiencing its ravages is one of the most difficult tasks you will ever experience.

If you experienced a sudden death, there are a number of possibilities of what you may be feeling.

Your capacity to cope may be diminished as the shock overwhelms you at the same time additional stressors enter your life. In addition, your loss doesn't make sense and can't be understood or absorbed, and why questions abound. This event usually leaves you with a sense of unreality that may last a long time.

Your symptoms of acute grief, and physical and emotional shock, may persist for a prolonged period of time.

A sudden death fosters a stronger-than-normal sense of guilt expressed in "If only..." statements. You may repeat these scenarios again and again.

You may feel an extremely strong need to blame someone for what happened.

You may feel a profound loss of security and confidence in your world, which may affect all areas of your life and increase many kinds of anxiety.

Sudden death often involves medical and legal authorities, and this can intensify and prolong your grieving.

Death cuts across all experiences in your relationship with your loved one and tends to highlight what was happening at the time of death. This often causes you to accentuate these last-minute situations out of proportion to the rest of the relationship.

Sudden death could leave you with many regrets and a sense of unfinished business. There's no chance to say goodbye, and no closure.

In the event of a sudden death, your need is to understand why it happened and ascribe not only the cause but also the blame. Sometimes God is the only available target, and it is not uncommon to hear someone who has lost a loved one say, "I hate God."

Because of the unexpected nature of the event, the death tends to be followed by a number of major secondary losses.

Your loved one may have been ill and dying over a prolonged period of time. If so, you probably experienced *anticipatory* grief. I experienced that in losing my wife, Joyce, who struggled with brain cancer for four years.

With a gradual death, each day can bring new losses. If you watched your loved one slowly change or became debilitated or lose control, your grief was for the current loss and also for the future that would never be. Anticipatory grief is both a mourning of what is occurring each day as well as what the future holds.

The word "anticipatory" means "to feel or realize beforehand; to look forward to or foresee and fulfill in advance." One of the most difficult times of life is when what we anticipate is the inevitability of someone's death. We tend to think of grief as after the fact rather than beforehand.

One wife said, "When all that remained was hope for my husband's survival, and he continued to decline, I felt absolutely helpless. My arsenal was depleted. There was nothing to do but surrender and redefine hope to be much greater than whether he lived or died. In the end, the effort to forestall seemed to cause everyone involved suffering. At the same time, it was an integral part of the journey."

Trepidation—"trepidatory" grief—would be a closer fit for the kind of grief people with a life-threatening illness and their loved ones go through up to the point where bad days outnumber the good ones.

In anticipatory grief, you may have had the opportunity to say and do things during the illness that helped the dying loved one and family members and friends.

In *How We Grieve,* author Thomas Attig describes the journey so well:

> We lose the continuing presence of those we care about and love. This is by no means a simple thing. We also lose the security and the coherence in our lives that were rooted in our expectation that those who died would continue to live. We lose any of the meaning and purpose in our lives that are rooted in our hopes and dreams for future life with the deceased by our sides. We do not lose any of the time lived with the deceased prior to the death. We lose none of what was given to us in our relationships. The meanings of the lives now ended are not canceled, as survivors, we can still incorporate the inspiration and influence of those who have died into our own lives.
>
> No matter how vivid our memories, not seeing those we care about and love, not hearing, not touching or holding, not sharing

laughter or tears, not conversing, not deciding together, not greeting or ending the day together, even not arguing in person render our memories painfully pale.[1]

When a loved one dies, you focus on what you lose. You rarely focus on what you do not lose. You feel the loss of a loved one's presence most acutely in your daily life. Every moment you're aware of the absence.

You have also lost the presence of this person in the ongoing story of your life.

But you haven't lost the years you lived with him or her; you have the past. You can continue to love and cherish the story of an earthly life that is now over. Your loved one's death does not cancel his or her life or your history together. As you relive and retell the stories again and again, you will discover something new each time. Events in your life will remind you of the person and his or her continuing importance to you. Your life was shaped by who this person was; who he or she was can move you, strengthen your values and make a difference in your world.

The first chapter you will read, "The World of Grief," is foundational to your understanding, no matter who you have lost. You may resist your grief, but I encourage you not to succumb to that desire. Embrace your grief and let it play out; it's the means for you to move forward in your life.

You may ask, "How will I know when my grief is over?" It's probably never really over, but you can see signs of progress. There are several other ways to see signs of healing. You can be confident that you have begun to heal when:
- You begin to look outside yourself at how others in your family are handling the loss.
- You no longer feel the need to escape from your emotions.
- You feel more comfortable about your grief and are willing to talk about it.
- You have a day without emotional stress.
- You can discuss, observe or experience memories (good and bad)

without having feelings that overwhelm you.
- You see your socially conditioned behavior return, and it feels comfortable.
- You realize that no matter what happened, you did the best you or anyone else could have done under the circumstances.
- You begin to see glimpses of new or renewed meaning in your life again.
- You begin planning for the future again.

I would encourage you to do two things: Read the entire book, even though some chapters may not seem as though they apply to you. There are suggestions in each chapter that could help you. Read the recommended books listed at the end of the chapters to help you continue to grow in your understanding of grief.

1

The World of Grief

Grief. We don't even like the word or the sound of it, yet it's spoken of many times in the Scriptures:

> I tell you the truth, you will weep and mourn while the world rejoices. You will grieve, but your grief will turn to joy (John 16:20).
>
> I weep with grief; my heart is heavy with sorrow; encourage and cheer me with your words (Ps. 119:28, *TLB*).

When a person moves into the world of grief, he or she enters a world of unpredictability, chaos and pain. Each person in grief will have his or her own unique experience of it, but there are many common threads attached to grief for all who mourn.

When in grief, the bottom falls out of your world; the solid footing you once had is gone. With each step you take, it feels more like a floorboard is tilting or you're walking in soft, pliable mud. The stability of yesterday's emotions gives way to feelings that are so raw and fragile that you think you're losing your mind. Grief takes the color out of life. Everything looks black and white.

Mourning is another part of the experience. This is the process where grief is expressed. It's a natural, God-given process of recovery. It's His gift to us to help us get through the pain. Everyone experiences grief, but mourning is a choice. A person cannot make his grief better; he cannot make it go away, fix it or just get over it.

Many word pictures have been created to describe the experience of grief. Often, when grievers read these words, they say, "Yes, that's exactly the way I feel. I thought I was the only one." They discover they're not alone. What they are feeling is normal grief.

One grieving father said:

> Grief is like a wave. It comes rolling in from a far-off place. I could no more push it back than if I were standing in the water at the beach. I could not fight the wave. It moved over me and under me and broke against me, but I could

never stop it. It arrived at its destination. It worked around me. The harder I fought it, the more exhausted I became. So it is with grief. If I tried to fight it, it would vanquish me. If I pushed it down it would stick in my soul and emerge as something else; depression, bitterness, exhaustion. If I yielded to the waves and let it carry me, however, it would take me to a new place.[1]

It's a fact that all waves run out of energy. As they move closer to the shore, their power is spent and they slowly bubble up to the edge of the sand. So it is with a wave of grief. It takes you to the top of the wave, and then the wave breaks, and you struggle in the froth of emotion.

Waves of grief also bring memories. Grief will expose who you really are inside. The more you stand and fight and rail against the wave, the more exhausted you become. It's an exercise in futility. But the more you accept it, hold out your arms to it and even embrace it, the more you will recover. You need to take a step that for many is difficult—you need to yield to your grief. You will need to let it do its work in your life, and mourn.

When you enter into grief, you've entered into the valley of shadows. There is nothing heroic or noble about grief. It's painful. It's work. It's a lingering process. But it is necessary for all kinds of losses. It has been labeled everything from intense mental anguish to acute sorrow to deep remorse.

Emotions You Will Come to Know Well

The grief process is made up of a multitude of emotions that seem out of control and often appear in conflict with one another. With each loss come bitterness, emptiness, apathy, love, anger, guilt, sadness, fear, self-pity and a feeling of helplessness.

Doug Manning, in his book *Don't Take My Grief Away,* described it this way:

> Right now your chest hurts—
> The numbness has worn off and
> real pain has replaced it.

You wonder if you will ever be well again.
A thousand questions flood your mind.
A thousand hurts pop up every day—

Every day you find a new thing to cause memories and bring tears.
You find it hard to sleep.
The awful loneliness seems to be there every moment of every day.
The finality of death leaves a hollow feeling all over your body.

Loneliness comes in only one size—Extra Large.[2]

Pain is a close companion to grief. The pain of grief can feel overwhelming. It's like a visitor that has long overstayed his welcome. No one is immune to pain, but everyone resists its intrusion.

Denial—Your Initial Buffer

There are several ways we attempt to resist the pain. Some fight the pain through denial. They say, "No, it isn't true," or they attempt to live as though nothing has happened. When they hear about the death, their first response is often, "No, that's not true. Tell me it isn't so!" or "You're mistaken." They are trying to absorb the news, but it takes time to filter the shock. This is normal.

The author of *A Grace Disguised* said about denial, "Ultimately it diminishes the capacity of their souls to grow bigger in response to pain."[3]

Denial serves as an emotional anesthesia and as a defense mechanism so that you will not be totally overwhelmed by the loss. Denial allows you to gradually comprehend the loss, which makes it more bearable.

The process of grief moves through several levels of denial. Each stage that brings home the reality of the loss is a bit deeper and more painful. In that first stage is acceptance of the loss in our heads, then in our feelings; and finally, we adjust life's pattern to reflect the reality of what has occurred. If we stay in denial for too long, we pay a price. The energy required to keep denial operating drains us and, in time, we can become damaged emotionally, delaying our recovery.

Denial is a cushion. We use denial to block out the unthinkable, but it brings with it fear of the unknown since we are denying the reality of what happened. As denial lessens, the pain begins to settle in; as it does, fear of the unknown diminishes.

Mental Confusion and Disruption

Grieving is also a disorderly process. It can't be controlled and it can't be scheduled. Grief takes the shape of a spiral figure rather than a linear one. Grief is not a straight line moving forward only to return one to where he or she used to be. One may think he or she has left behind that intense pain only to revisit it again before relief is rediscovered. This cycle can repeat itself again and again.

Grief disrupts the mind and a person's thinking ability. Confusion moves in and memory takes a vacation. If you suffer short-term memory loss after a death, it's probably a result of the stress and anxiety you are experiencing. Your life has been paralyzed and shut down. The more quickly you accept what is occurring to you, the sooner it will pass.

You may even experience your last interaction with the person who died. Some people say the experience is so real that it's as though they are actually talking with the deceased person again. These experiences will pass. They're normal responses to loss.

You may find yourself easily distracted and perhaps disoriented even if you're usually decisive. Now you may be afraid to make choices.

Many people find that their sense of time is distorted. Time passes too quickly or too slowly. Past and future collapse together. Even if a clock is sitting in front of them, time doesn't register. Recently, a grieving mother said that she was in a time warp, frozen in time.

Grief is one of the most uncomfortable places to ever reside. It hurts, confuses, upsets and frightens anyone who is living with it.

Whenever there is loss, there will be grief. But some people do not grieve or mourn; they make a choice to repress all the feelings inside of them, so their grief accumulates. Saving it up won't lessen grief's pain; it will only intensify it. Silence covers a wound before the cleansing has occurred. The result is an emotional infection. Perhaps you, or a family member, have experienced the result of unexpressed grief.

Some people try to make others carry their burden. But grief can't be shared. Everyone has to carry it alone, and carry it in his or her own way.[4]

Grief Has No Schedule

The grief process is slow and it needs to be this way, even though most people probably want to rush it along. It will take longer than anyone has patience for. Time seems to stand still, especially at night; but the slowness of grief's passage is a necessary thing.

Everyone grieves and heals differently. Some people want to be connected to other people as much as possible; some prefer to be left alone. Some prefer to take care of their own problems, while others want assistance. One person may prefer activity, while another seeks just the opposite. And some may even attempt to fill their lives with what they don't want.

It will take effort, but you may need to let others know what you need and the best way for them to help you. When grief is your close companion, you experience it in many ways. It permeates and changes your feelings, thoughts and attitudes.

Why does everyone have to go through this experience? What is its purpose?

- Through grief, you express your feelings about the loss.
- Through grief, you express your protest at the loss, as well as your desire to change what happened and have it not be true. This is a normal response.
- Through grief, you express the effects you have experienced from the devastating impact of the loss.[5]
- Through grief, you may experience God in a new way that changes your

life. As Job said, "My ears had heard of you before, but now my eyes have seen you" (Job 42:5, *NCV*).

During seasons of grief, the days may seem like night, and often with a blanket of fog covering everything. The psalmist reflected this when he said, "When my spirit was overwhelmed within me" (Ps. 142:3, *KJV*). These words literally mean, "The muffling of my spirit." But as grief begins to thaw, you will find the sun breaking through your gloom. The psalmist said, "Weeping may remain for a night, but rejoicing comes in the morning" (Ps. 30:5).

Perhaps one of the best descriptions of grief comes from Joanne T. Jozefowski's book *The Phoenix Phenomenon: Rising from the Ashes of Grief.* These characteristics or symptoms with such a fitting title seem to resonate with almost everyone I've shared them with; and all too often, I hear, "Yes. Every one of these symptoms describes what my life is like right now."

The "crazy" feelings of grief are actually a sane response to grief:

- Distorted thinking patterns, crazy and/or irrational thoughts, fearful thoughts
- Feelings of despair and hopelessness
- Out-of-control or numbed emotions
- Changes in sensory perceptions (sight, taste, smell)
- Increased irritability
- A desire to talk a lot or not at all
- Memory lags and mental short circuits
- Inability to concentrate
- Obsessive focus on the loved one
- Losing track of time
- Increase or decrease of appetite and/or sexual desire
- Difficulty falling or staying asleep
- Dreams in which the deceased seems to visit the griever
- Nightmares in which death themes are repeated
- Physical illness like the flu, headaches or other maladies
- Shattered beliefs about life, the world and even God

The passage of grief will take longer than you could ever imagine. It tends to intensify after three months, on special dates and on the one-year anniversary.[6]

Why Is Everything Changing?

Grief takes on many faces—disruption, a feeling of emptiness, confusion. It disrupts one's entire life schedule. Grief doesn't leave one particle of life untouched; it is all consuming. And there are physical changes. Food doesn't taste the same; the fragrance of a favorite flower is not as intense. The frequency of tears clouds vision. Some experience a tightness of breath or rapid heart rate. Eating and sleeping patterns will be different. Some people sleep and sleep, while others wish that sleep would come. Sleep is either an easy escape or it's elusive. Dreams or nightmares occur. This disruption will decrease in time, but recovery is not a smooth, straightforward path; it's a forward-backward dance.

If your grief results from the death of a loved one, your life has now been divided into two segments—life before the death and life after. Grief can also bring out the best in you, as well as the worst.

Life was going in a well-established direction prior to the death of your loved one. Before the death, you could say who the person was as part of your identity. This has changed. You are not exactly who you were. The person who died was someone's mother or aunt or spouse or brother. He or she continues to be that person in your heart and memory, but there's a vacant place where he or she once stood. The loss of this person has subtracted part of who you were.

Am I Going Crazy?

You may also experience the "face in the crowd" syndrome. You think you have seen the one you lost, or heard his or her voice, or smelled his or her perfume or cologne. This can happen at home or in public places. You may wake up at night and swear you sensed the person's presence in the room or heard him or her call your name. You think you're going crazy and hesitate to share the experience with others for fear of what they will think. This experience is more common than most realize and can last for as long as 18 months.

It is not just the loss of a loved one that is so painful. It is also all the other losses that occur because he or she has died; the way the person lived, loved, slept, ate, worked and worshiped—all areas are affected. Often the death of the loved one brings up more than grief for what has been lost; it also brings up what the person never had and never will have.

There is a loss of the present as well as the future. This especially impacts relationships. You may feel awkward around others for whom the one they lost was also a loved one. A death can put distance in some relationships or draw together and connect others in a greater intimacy than before. Death can be a wedge or source of confusion. You may feel disconnected with others, alienated, and you may tend to withdraw, which reinforces those feelings. This can lead to a belief that "others just don't understand," which is often true.

How Do I Let Go?

Processing the grief involves saying goodbye to the old life. This occurs by acknowledging that the loved one is truly gone and won't return. Many people struggle with holding on while trying to let go. The ongoing task is to develop a new way of relating to the one who has died.

One way to say goodbye to the one you loved is to share with him or her what you wanted to say and perhaps didn't. Sometimes, you may wish you could communicate with your loved one again. What I recommend, and have done myself, is to write a letter to the person who has died and have it laminated, then read it aloud at the place of interment and leave it there. Here is one of several letters I wrote to my wife, Joyce, a year after her death.

August 22, 2008
Dear Joyce,

It's hard to believe it's been almost a year since you left my side. In some ways it seems forever, but I know it won't be forever, since I'll see you again. What will that be like? What is heaven really like? You would know, and you looked forward to it so much. I have more questions about heaven now than before. As I write this, I'm sitting at my desk eating (what else?) a chocolate chip cookie, and I feel your presence here. It's like you're looking at me out of this picture when you sat with Shaelyn at the little table. Your eyes were bright and your pleasant smile was radiant. I'm so glad I have this picture as a reminder. There's an empty place in my life, and I know it will always be there. Sometimes it expands and then shrinks, but it's ever present.

You ministered so much to people when you were here, and in your homegoing you continue to impact lives. You are not and never will be forgotten. Sheryl misses you *so* much. I ache for her as well.

I'm so thankful for the 48 years we had together. I wish you were by my side today on our forty-ninth. God was so gracious in giving us such a special evening last year. You were so alert, and even hungry. We had the Petroleum Club to ourselves, and the staff was so attentive and gracious to us. You even wanted another one of those special desserts they prepared for you! I am so thankful for our memories.

I read some of the cards again today. One said, "Joyce Wright: Humble caregiver. Joy was a hero. She was a servant and was a joy to anyone who passed by her life. When I think about this lovely lady who now walks the streets of heaven, I think of her entry to her celestial home—meeting her Savior who said, 'Well done, my faithful servant.'" This was echoed by so many.

There are times when I've cried out, "Joyce, why did you have to leave!" I know why. I understand. But ... God is using this experience to change and refine me and to minister to others in grief.

I wish I could hear you, see you and touch you again. It's difficult to write now, since I wrote so much during the first few months. But I always want to write to you.

Perhaps one of my journal entries can sum up what's in my heart.

Thank you for:
- who you were as a person
- influencing and enriching my life in such a positive way
- being such a model of graciousness
- your love and faithfulness to the Word of God
- what you gave to Matthew, Sheryl and Shaelyn
- loving me with a sacrificial love
- fulfilling my life in a way I never dreamed possible
- impacting thousands of people by who you were as much as by what you said, and this is continuing
- giving to me memories, which will last forever

"Thank you" will continue. And one day the difficult word "goodbye"

will no longer be expressed. It, too, will be replaced by "Hello, Joyce."
I love you forever,
Norm

Why Can't I Feel Anything?

Grief brings behavioral changes. You may say, "I'm just not myself." That's true. You won't be for some time. You may find yourself zoning out when others are talking; your mind drifts off because it's difficult to stay focused and attentive. You feel detached from people and activities even though they're an important part of your life. What is upsetting to many is how absentminded you are. You may cry for no apparent reason. It's common to lose your sense of awareness of where you are, relating both to time and place.

Whether the death was expected or sudden, you may experience numbness. The more unexpected and traumatic the loss, the more intense the numbness will be. At first, your feelings are muted, like muting the sound on a TV. The initial shock of knowing that a loved one is dead puts most people into a paralyzing state of shock. This is a period in which no one experiencing it can describe things clearly, thanks to nature's protective measures. Shock is a natural protection, as though someone gave you anesthesia. It insulates you from the intensity of the feelings of loss, but it also may prevent you from understanding the full experience of the loss.

Why Do I Feel Even Worse Now?

There will come a time when feelings can be described as a time of suffering and disorganization or even chaos. The trance is over. We talk about scenes rather than stages. And there are those who bypass some scenes. After the numbness wears off, the pain of separation comes. Sometimes those who grieve wish they could go back to the initial stage of numbness or shock. At least then the pain wasn't so intense.

There is an intense longing for the return of the person who was lost—for the sight of them, the sound of them, their smell, and just knowing he or she could walk through the door again. One person described the loss of a loved one as "like having a tree that has been growing in one's heart yanked out by its roots, leaving a gaping hole or wound."[7] And the why question begins to form. Perhaps that is where you are right now.

You may ask or even shout "Why?" countless times a day at this point. And you may wonder, *Do I have the right to ask why?* It's not just a question; it's a heart-wrenching cry of protest. It's the reaction, "No, this shouldn't be! It isn't right!"

Job, in the Bible, asked that question 16 times. And there are others in Scripture. Listen to their cries.

> Why, O LORD, do you stand far off? Why do you hide yourself in times of trouble? (Ps. 10:1).

> > How long, O LORD? Will you forget me forever? How long will you hide your face from me? How long must I wrestle with my thoughts and every day have sorrow in my heart? How long will

my enemy triumph over me? (Ps. 13:1-2).

Ken Gire wrote, "Painful questions, all of them. Unanswered questions, many of them. And if we live long enough and honestly enough, one day we will ask them, too."[8]

It's not unusual to struggle to pray. At times it's as though the words stick in your mind and can't get past your lips. The questions, concerns, pleas and requests are there, but they derail when you attempt to express them to God.

You Can Expect to Feel Clusters of Emotions

Emotions come in clusters and are a normal part of the grieving process. One of the clusters of feelings to emerge will be a sense of emptiness, loneliness and isolation, even when others are next to you in your grief. Invisible boundaries have been erected. In two or three months' time, there will be even more loneliness and isolation as friends and family naturally pull away from you.

Fear and Anxiety

The second common cluster of feelings is fear and anxiety. And the fears accumulate. They may come and go or manifest as a constant sense of dread and are a common response whenever we face the unknown and the unfamiliar. These feelings range from the fear of being alone to fear of the future, fear of additional loss, and fear of desertion or abandonment.

Fear works as an alarm system that warns us of major changes in our understanding and assumptions regarding ourselves and others.[9] Anxiety awakens an awareness of our inability to control events. It's common to feel that you should have been able to prevent or at least predict the occurrence of the loss. "What will I do?" is a phrase that expresses fear. The greater the emotional investment in the one who was lost, the more you will tend to feel like a ship adrift at sea.

One fear may be that if you stop wanting the person to return, it means you have stopped loving him or her. In addition, the worst agony of intense grief occurs when you realize that the return you want more than anything else is the one you can't have.[10]

Some have said, "You need to let go of the loved one completely." But consider the thinking of the author of *The Heart of Grief:*

> Grieving persons who want their loved ones back need to look for some other way to love them while they are apart. Desperate longing prevents their finding that different way of loving. Letting go of having them with us in the flesh is painful and necessary. But it is not the same as completely letting go. We still hold the gifts they gave us, the values and meanings we found in their lives. We can love them as we cherish their memories we found in their lives. We can love them as we treasure their legacies in our practical lives, and spirits. But there is nothing in all of this that implies that we must let go completely. There is no reason to let go of the good with the bad.[11]

You may wake up and ask, "How can I face the day without him (without her)?" You are afraid of being on your own. You may feel anxious over dealing with the pain of the separation. You may feel upset over the realization that you are a different person now. You're without someone. Many people in grief worry over how other family members will cope and survive. Since you've lost one person, what if you lose another family member or friend, especially if the current loss was sudden and unexpected?

Guilt, Shame and Regret

Another cluster of feelings, guilt, shame and regret, walk their way into the grief process. There are numerous sources for the guilt. The most immediate guilt comes from taking some responsibility for the loss; or perhaps guilt is connected to a discussion that you feel contributed to the loss in some way. Guilt is possibly the most difficult emotion to handle. It's often tied to unrealistic expectations. Some who are in grief hold themselves responsible for events over which they had no control, such as thinking they could have done something differently or done something more to prevent the death. Guilt could also be leftover unfinished business, and it leads to regret that turns into guilt.

Some continue to live in the land of regret and let their lives become a continuous self-recriminating statement. And these regrets seem to grow: "I should have said ... I should have done ... I should have known..." Guilt may result from unresolved negative feelings over things done or not done.

Survivor Guilt and Anger

In the early phases of grief, it's common to recall all that was negative in a relationship while failing to remember the positive. Another tendency may be for a person to dwell on all the bad or negative things he thinks he did in his relationship with the deceased person while also focusing on all the good things the deceased did. And then there is survivor guilt. The person in grief feels guilty because he or she is still alive.

Guilt is an unpredictable emotion, and that alone creates guilt. Some experience guilt because they are not recovering according to their expected timetable. This is where self-talk that uses the words "should" and "if only" come to mind. When a death was unexpected or came sooner than anticipated, the tendency can be to blame others first. From there it's easy to transfer the blame to self: "If only I had..." Self-recrimination can be endless. And if suicide was the cause of death, this feeling can be overwhelming.

Anger, in general, is an emotion of displeasure, irritation and protest when feeling frustrated, hurt, afraid or helpless. Anger/hostility acts as a protective self-defense emotion that demands that the world be predictable and operate according to one's expectations. Sometimes anger is expressed like a heat-seeking missile. It can erupt suddenly without warning.

Anger is a common response to hurt or pain. Anger in grief is often a protest, a desire to make someone pay, to declare the unfairness of the death. Anger can be an expression of pain in the past, the present or the future.

When the pain is in the past, anger takes the form of resentment. It's not uncommon to experience these feelings even toward the one who died. When direct expression is blocked, it leaks out and gets invested elsewhere. If it is invested against oneself, it can turn into depression.

Some people may find it especially difficult to admit being angry at God, perhaps when He has not responded in the way the person wanted, or because the person's faith and beliefs didn't seem to work. This kind of distress, when God does not respond in a desired way, can prolong the grief process.

Sadness, Depression and Despair

Finally, there is the sense of sadness, depression and despair. Depression makes each day look as though the dark clouds are here to stay. Apathy blankets the person like a shroud, and withdrawal becomes a lifestyle. When depression hits, an accurate perception leaves. Depression will alter relationships because the one in grief is oversensitive to what others say and do. Jeremiah the prophet displayed these feelings: "Desperate is my wound. My grief is great. My sickness is incurable, but I must bear it" (Jer. 10:19, *TLB*). The deeper the depression, the more paralyzing is a person's sense of helplessness. Depression can also affect us spiritually and change the way we see God.

Some have said that grief is the blackout night of confusion because of all the many varieties of emotion associated with it. The range of feelings is like a smorgasbord—each day bringing a wide variety to choose from. And there will be daily variations of emotions that come and go. Just when you think a particular emotion is gone for good, it comes again and overlaps the others. Over time, these emotions come less frequently and less intensely. This is why the "Ball of Grief" illustration is so helpful to visualize.

It's true that we can hold back and bottle up feelings, but not for long. If we don't let those feelings out, they will find their own means of expression.

Is Feeling Relief Normal?

One of the secret feelings of grief is relief. Few would admit to this. It's an "I shouldn't be experiencing this" kind of feeling.

One of the struggles when in grief is wondering if it's all right to feel and think what we are feeling and thinking. We know what we're experiencing, but we wonder if it's okay and hope that it is with those around us. To assist you in identifying your emotions, look at the "Ball of Grief" graphic each day to identify where you are, since feelings come and go.

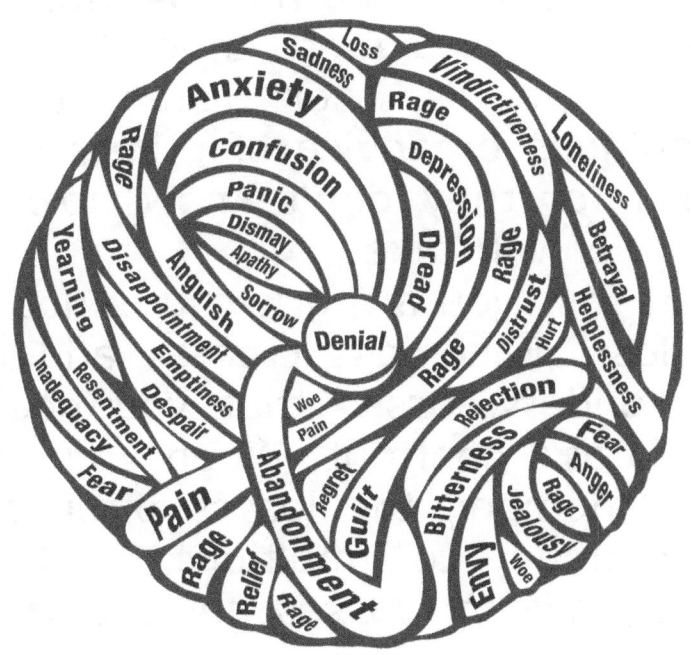

Ball of Grief

When it comes to understanding grief, there are several factors to keep in mind that may ease some of the pressure you put on yourself.

First of all, even though grief is as normal as a cold, it's not an illness that needs a prescription or surgery. Everyone grieves differently, and there isn't one right way to grieve. Never compare your grief with another's; your grief is uniquely your own.

Your grief schedule will be unique. It will take as long as it needs to take, and that, too, is normal. Again, don't compare your grief timetable with someone else's, nor listen to the admonitions or advice of others in this regard, for they don't know how long your grief will take.

The loss you are grieving is not your only loss. Each loss creates additional or secondary losses that you need to identify and confront. When you lose a family member, the losses often seem to continue to multiply, and you wonder, *Will the losses never end?*

With each new loss, you may experience a previous loss of a loved one even though you felt you had completed your grieving. Old grief can mingle with your current grief.[12]

When you are in grief, you want others to accept and understand where you are and not try to fix you, for you don't need to be fixed. You're not broken. When you're sad, you want to know that it's all right. Sorrow is not an enemy. Your grief keeps you close to the one you lost. If you have lost a close loved one, isn't he or she worthy of sorrow? Your feelings will fluctuate; there will be a time for laughter, and this is appropriate. Nancy Guthrie wrote:

> Sometimes we are afraid to laugh lest people think our pain has passed or that our sorrow has been a sham. But just as tears give vent to the deep sorrow we feel, laughter reveals that while grief may have a grip on us, it hasn't choked the life out of us. Laughter takes some of the sting out of hurt. It gives us perspective and relieves the pressure.[13]

Do you find yourself not wanting to interact with others? It's all right to want to be alone; other people don't have to understand. You may need to be alone with your grief. But it's also all right to want to be with others, especially if you were involved as a caregiver for a period of time. You may need the comfort and support or just be in the presence of others. Other people can help by listening or sharing their own memories. It's also perfectly all right not to talk about the deceased and to engage in discussions of anything you would like to talk about.

When you're in grief, your vulnerability and greatest weakness may rise to the surface. You're not your usual self; you can't be and won't be. Just assert this and lean upon others and the Lord. Your main source of joy, as well as strength, is in the Lord.

There will be days when you will surprise yourself by the strength and stability you feel. Just remember that this doesn't mean that your grief is over. It's just a break from your grief, which will return. So when someone asks how you're doing, you have a wide variety of responses to give. These are *your* responses. This is *you* in grief, and you can be free to share this with others.[14]

Give Yourself Permission

A long recovery does not mean you did or didn't love as much as you thought you did. You will react to grief and recover from grief just like you react to all other things in life. You have your own timetable. Recovery may take years. It may take much longer. There is no set timetable for grief recovery.

Not only do some people not give you the time to recover, but the problem also may be that *you* do not give *yourself* time to recover. *You* may be the greatest source of pressure. It may be you who feels that your faith is not strong if you are not well within a period of weeks. It may be you who tries to take your grief away.

You must give yourself permission to grieve. You are going to grieve whether or not you give yourself permission to do so. The difference is that if you do not give yourself permission, you will be in a state of war within yourself during the grieving process. If you do give yourself permission, you can relax and not fight against yourself or the grief process.

To fight against yourself adds tension and hurt to the grief. To fight against yourself takes away energy that is desperately needed for grief recovery. To fight against yourself can lead you to act well long before you are well. Acting well is not being well. By acting well, you will lengthen the grief process. You may even have a relapse later when acting well becomes too much to bear.

You give yourself permission to grieve by recognizing the need for grieving. Grieving is the natural way of working through the loss of a loved one. It is not weakness or absence of faith. It is as natural as crying when you hurt, sleeping when you are tired or sneezing when your nose itches. It is nature's way of healing a broken heart.

When you are in grief, you are in one of the most painful experiences of your life. What you are facing will leave you feeling vulnerable, exhausted and weak. The best response for you at this time is to treat yourself as if you were in an intensive care unit. Your focus is on yourself and no one else. You need to care for yourself, and that is not selfish. Grieving is a time of convalescence.

Grief is not an enemy; it is a friend. It is the natural process of walking through hurt and growing because of the walk. Let it happen. Stand up tall to friends and to yourself and say, "Don't take my grief away from me. I deserve it, and I am going to have it."[15]

This suggestion may sound strange, but it's all right to practice saying no to others. Many people are going to try to fix you. But you don't need to be fixed, since you're not broken. Some are going to be impatient with your grieving journey. You are not grieving for anyone else to feel comfortable. It's not for their benefit, but for yours. When you hear advice or suggestions or requests from others, just say that you need to think about it and you will let them know. It's a polite way of saying no.

You don't need to be concerned about hurting someone else at this time. The other individual may be grieving for the same one you lost, but the one you need to take care of right now is you. You probably don't even have enough energy for that. If you've been the one that others have always leaned on, this will be a big adjustment for them, but a necessary one. You may need to receive the help of others rather than give help, but consider carefully the offers of others to help you. Sometimes you end up feeling drained rather than replenished.

To reduce pressure from others in having to explain what you are experiencing, you may want to print a card or letter to give out when others ask, and also post it on Facebook. Here is an example of one we used prior to my wife's homegoing:

> Greetings,
>
> Joyce was not able to accompany me to this conference. The reason for this is on January 6, Joyce underwent a craniotomy,

at Cedars Sinai Hospital in Los Angeles, because of a tumor on the left temporal lobe of her brain, which is the area for speech. It had originated within the brain itself and the risk for removal was too great. A biopsy was performed, and both the immediate as well as the complete analysis indicated stage-2 cancer called glioma.

The best treatment option, because of the tumor's location, is chemotherapy. Since January, Joyce has had a series of five rounds using a pill form called Temodar. The side effects have been nausea and loss of energy. The chemo is taken at home and is a five-day process each month.

Last month, Joyce underwent another MRI, and on Thursday we had a consultation with the doctors at Cedar Sinai. They were both pleased and surprised with the progress since the tumor is continuing to shrink. Most of the research and clinical trials have been with stage-4 tumors using Temodar. Therefore, the medical staff didn't know what to expect using this chemo with a stage-2 tumor.

In a sense it would appear that Joyce is part of an experiment and everyone is pleased with the progress. She continues to use Dilantin, a seizure medication, as a precaution. In either three or six months of continued chemo, it appears that radiation treatments might be used to completely eradicate this tumor.

We deeply appreciate all the words of encouragement and prayers from so many. This is a new journey that we did not expect, but we're not traveling alone. God's Word is even more real and precious at this time. Old verses have become new and fresh. We are walking day by day with a greater appreciation for each moment. And we're so glad to be living close to Sheryl, Bill and Shaelyn.

Thank you for your support.

Norm Wright

"God is our refuge and strength, an ever-present help in trouble. Therefore we will not fear" (Ps. 46:1-2).

Sleep can be difficult when you're grieving, but it is essential to your health. A continued lack of sleep will make it difficult to deal with your emotions. They may rage out of control. Here are several suggestions that have worked for many in this area of sleep. Some people want to dream about their loved one, while others do not. Most people like to remember their dreams. If that is you, you may want to keep a dream journal. As soon as you wake up, spend a few minutes writing down what you can remember. Do this before you get out of bed. Start with any fragment of the dream and then try to reconstruct it. Put a pad of paper and a pen by your bed and remind yourself before going to sleep that you will remember your dreams.

If you have repetitive nightmares, prior to going to sleep recall the details of the nightmare and change the ending to one that is positive. Write it out and read it out loud. This suggestion has helped many.

If you are struggling with falling asleep, or you wake up and have difficulty getting back to sleep, read the following Scriptures aloud, and make them a personal prayer by changing the pronouns to first person, just before you turn out the light:

> When you lie down you shall not be afraid; yes, you shall lie down, and your sleep shall be sweet. Be not afraid of sudden terror *and* panic, nor of the stormy blast *or* the storm and ruin of the wicked when it comes [for you will be guiltless], For the Lord shall be your confidence, firm *and* strong, and shall keep your foot from being caught [in a trap or some hidden danger] (Prov. 3:24-26, *AMP*).

> You will not be afraid when you go to bed, and you will sleep soundly through the night (Prov. 3:24, *GNB*).

> If I'm sleepless at midnight, I spend the hours in grateful reflection (Ps. 63:6, *THE MESSAGE*).

> When my anxious thoughts multiply within me, Your

consolations delight my soul (Ps. 94:19, *NASB*).

I will lie down and sleep in peace, for you alone, O Lord, make me dwell in safety (Ps. 4:8).

Do not be afraid of the terrors of the night (Ps. 91:5, *NLT*).
In a dream, a vision of the night
When sound sleep falls on men,...
Then He opens the ears of men,
And seals their instruction (Job 33:15-16, *NASB*).

You might also find it helpful to read the following prayer aloud:

Dear God,

We give thanks for the darkness of the night where lies the world of dreams. Guide us closer to our dreams so that we may be nourished by them. Give us good dreams and memory of them so that we may carry their poetry and mystery into our daily lives.

Grant us deep and restful sleep that we may wake refreshed with strength enough to renew a world grown tired.

We give thanks for the inspiration of stars, the dignity of the moon and the lullabies of crickets and frogs.

Let us restore the night and reclaim it as a sanctuary of peace, where silence shall be music to our hearts and darkness shall throw light upon our souls. Good night. Sweet dreams.

Amen.[16]

Recommended Resources

H. Norman Wright, *Experiencing Grief* (Nashville, TN: B&H Books, 2004).

Nancy Guthrie, *Hearing Jesus Speak into Your Sorrow* (Carol Stream, IL: Tyndale House Publishers, 2009).

2

The Loss of a Spouse

Your future has abruptly changed. In one sense, you believed life together would go on forever. But grief has dropped a curtain over that belief. It's difficult to imagine the future when you're trapped in a fog. To envision a future you need to make some forward progress and avoid getting permanently stuck in a quagmire. But the clarity and anticipation you once knew have faded into uncertainty. The dreams you once had included a companion at your side, and now there's just an empty space.

Your mind tells you many messages: *He (or she) is with the Lord, and I'll be all right. The future is still there and bright. I will heal in time. I can do it.* But your heart says something quite different, and grief short-circuits your mind and heart's attempt to work together.

Perhaps you are saying, "The future? Yes, but what kind? What will it be like?" And yet, you direct little energy toward considering the future; it is evasive and painful to contemplate because of the empty space within its image. Consider these words of a grieving spouse:

> I wish I could tell you that the pain you feel today will be gone in six months, or one, or three ... and then no more tears, no more sorrow, no more lonely days.
>
> I can't.

"How long after your spouse has died will you mourn, and hurt, in tumultuous confusion? When can you expect to begin to feel normal? And, please, please ... when will the emotional pain go away?" These questions will haunt you time and time again. I'd love to offer a precise timetable for you.

No one can you give you an exact time.

Typically, family and friends who have not experienced anything like what you and I have in losing a spouse hold to an impression that we should have our lives back together in short order, within a few, quick months.

When you married your spouse, the words, "until death do us part," were said as a matter of course, borne of tradition. But we really give little thought to the phrase. That concept is buried in our minds as the feelings of love and our future companionship consume us.

Life's experiences prepare us to cope with many things, including some preparation for the death of a loved one. But we can do so little to prepare for the grief we feel when that death occurs.

The loss of a spouse causes dramatic and immediate changes in every part of your life, affecting, usually threatening, the very fabric of your existence. Each person brings very special qualities to the marriage union. If you are like me, and I imagine that most people are, you took for granted so much of what your spouse provided.

You, perhaps, never realized or appreciated how much your spouse brought to the partnership. Unfortunately, in grimness and probably tugged by regret and guilt, now you are discovering how significant these contributions were.[1]

When you lose a loved one, almost everything in you and around you changes at the moment of death. Or it seems to. You feel isolated. And you may feel as if the world is now a vast, confusing and chaotic place. You long for just a few moments with your loved one. You reflect on the happiness your mate brought to your life. Nothing else makes sense to you, because the rare and meaningful relationship you cherished is now gone. Consumed by the devastating loss and your longing, you see yourself and the world much differently than before. *From this time on,* you think, *the world will never be the same.* And in a very real sense, your world *was* changed the moment your loved one died. Each person you love makes up a precious and vital place of your world. At such a challenging time, you need to be patient with the chaos you are now enduring inside and around you.[2]

You have to adjust to function without the interaction and validation you were accustomed to receiving from your spouse. The lack of your loved one's presence means many things. Your needs, hopes, dreams, expectations, feelings and thoughts are forced to change. Slowly, over time, the reality of separation sinks in, and you realize, *Now I exist without my partner. I'm living without my mate.* You live without.

Relearning How to Live

As you reside in a world characterized by without—without the one you loved in every aspect of your life—you feel pain. You need to relearn who you will be without the other, and how you will function. You need to relearn yourself, since you lose part of yourself when you lose your spouse. You need to adjust your relationships with others and perhaps even with God, just as Job did. Remember, after his losses and trauma he cried out, "My ears had heard of you but now my eyes have seen you" (Job 42:5). Now you are relearning and reshaping your daily life. You don't get back to normal. You find your way to a purposeful, meaningful and hopeful life again. You make choices for the present and the future to avoid becoming a prisoner of the past. Yes, it's painful and may take longer than you imagine.

The loss of your spouse changes your entire life. It shifts the foundation of your existence. Nothing is as it was. Even the familiar becomes unfamiliar. Every aspect of your life is disrupted without your partner. Everything has to be relearned, just as a flooded river does when it recedes and leaves behind a maze of new streams.

In a culture that doesn't like to acknowledge loss or talk about its impact, grieving a loss is difficult. And when you add this silence to the fact that most of us have never been taught about the process and normalcy of grief, no wonder we struggle.

Prior to the death of your spouse, your life was going in a well-established direction. You had an identity. You could say who you were. This has now changed. You're not exactly who you were. The person you lost was part of your identity. You were someone's spouse, someone's partner. You continue to be that person in your heart and memory, but there's a vacant place where your loved one stood.

There was a time when your world consisted of you and your spouse. You probably didn't realize just how much he or she was your life, but now you're aware all too much. There's a hole in your personal life, as well as in your daily routine and schedule. Now you feel alone.

All the activities you shared together must now be done in isolation—or at least it feels that way. What was shared can now only be shared in memory, and you enter into the world of without. It's as though you have entered a train station with two different sets of tracks and a train on each one. Most engines have names, as did these two. One was named "Without" and the other was named "Blessings." At this time, the Without train is raging and has a full head of steam, ready to move in a second. The Blessings train is sitting quietly. Every now and then it may let out a tiny puff of steam, but the other train is the one that forges ahead.

Someday, one day, the Without train and its energy will begin to diminish. Its wheels will slow and its momentum will fade. Slowly, ever so slowly, it will fall behind its counterpart, and eventually the Blessings train will catch up with and pass the Without train. The past will become a distant speck.

Once in a while, Without may forge ahead again, but it can't sustain its former pace. For some reason it has to make its presence known. Perhaps it comes because some of the memories have dimmed and there's a subconscious fear of forgetting the one who was loved. The train's momentum is a cry to the memory of the loved one. "See, you haven't been forgotten—and you never will be!" Then the Without train falls behind again. And perhaps, someday, its wheels will slow even more, even grinding to a stop. A great sigh will come from the engine as it rests. Without has accepted that you're moving on in life. Its presence is no longer because someday "without" will be replaced by "together again."

When your spouse dies unexpectedly, the last time you were

together is very significant. You remember the last conversation, the last touch and the surroundings. Everything about that time stands out vividly. It's as though somebody hit a "freeze" button and the movie of your life stopped at that instant. You play it over and over in your mind.

If your last memory was pleasant, grieving is easier. The good memory comforts you. But it doesn't always happen that way. You may have wanted to be with your spouse when he or she died, but the suddenness of the event robbed you of the opportunity. You may have wanted to say more to your mate the last time you were together. Or your last encounter could have been an unpleasant conflict, and the relationship hadn't been fully restored yet. There's a feeling of unfinished business. When you parted, you thought, *We'll work this out tonight, or tomorrow.* But tomorrow never had a chance to arrive.

The last unpleasant scene may tend to haunt you. Your task then is to soften the memories and images that hurt you so much. How do you do this? By doing some editing just as if your life were a movie. You can hang on to the hurting, negative images or choose to go back a bit further in time and dwell on a scene that is representative of your overall relationship. That scene can become your source of comfort since it more accurately represents the relationship you had.[3]

This journey of grief and being alone involves relearning your world—a world drastically changed by the death of your spouse. What you experience now will never be experienced the way it was before. The life patterns and daily routines you once had exist no longer. You can't do what you used to do in the same way or get back everything you had at one time. Changes have been forced upon you. Like it or not, you've been put back in school to relearn what was once familiar and automatic but now has different nuances or is completely changed.

What will you need to relearn? Your physical surroundings. The rooms and furniture are reminders of your mate, as is your residence. There will be good memories that are comforting as well as painful ones you wish you could avoid. What do you leave out, and what do you put away, and when? What do you keep, and what do you dispose of? What about clothing worn on special occasions; colognes and perfumes; the bed you shared; the car; furniture your spouse loved and you hated; gifts you gave and gifts you received? What about your ring? All these entail decisions that need to be faced—but not immediately.

Your personal relationships need to be relearned; for they, too, will experience upheavals. You are different, and so are most people you know.

You'll also need to relearn who *you* are. Your identity and place in the world have changed. You have to adapt your daily routine and activities. Your hopes, dreams, desires and expectations have experienced a forced upheaval. Who are you now that you are alone? And what do you call yourself? Single? Widow(er)?

When your spouse died, you lost more than your spouse. Perhaps the next major loss was your sense of identity. "Who am I now?" will be an ongoing and unfolding question. Your sense of self as well as your sense of security have been impacted. The person you lost validated you in a certain way, and you have lost the one whose relationship caused you to be you.

Your spouse probably helped you to make sense of the world and the things in it. You may also have lost a person who perceived the world in the way you did and was also the one with whom you defined your world and self. For most of us, our spouse was the one of whom we could say, "She [or he] really knew me." Your spouse also provided you with a strong sense of history and special times. The one who could reminisce and remember with you is no longer around.

During your marriage, you probably thought of yourself as a "we" in your mind and heart. But now there is only an "I." One-half of you is gone. You are going to make the adjustment ofoperating in the world as one-half of a pair. The secondary losses and the losses created by the death of your spouse are many.

Consider these other losses:

Secondary Losses

friend	provider	handyman
cook	lover	bill payer
gardener	laundry person	companion
confidant(e)	sports partner	mentor
checkbook balancer	prayer partner	mechanic
	identity	encourager
source of inspiration or insight	counselor	teacher
	motivator	errand person
business partner	protector	couple friends
organizer	tax preparer	financial
adjustment	in-law support	couple's class
social adjustment	feeling of safety	

What additional losses are you experiencing?

How do we deal with this void? What can we do? We can broaden our roles and our skills and learn to function without our mate. We can learn to make up for what we lost. We change what we do and take on the responsibilities our spouse handled. There will be some things we give up, that we choose not to do anymore. Adjustment means not behaving the same way we did when our partner was an active part of our world.

For many, the loss of a spouse means acquiring a new identity. You will never be quite the same as you were before the loss. As one person said, "That portion of my life is history. I will never be that way or be that person again." You won't do or say what you used to, and sometimes the inability to do this hurts.

Who am I now? is an underlying question that most of us confront when our spouses die. We are not the same. We've changed.

Your spouse's death caused a massive shift in what you did, what you will do and who you are for now. You are no longer part of a couple. The more your life revolved around being married, the greater your discomfort will be. Your roles are now different, as are your responsibilities. Your "label," for lack of a better word, is different. Your time, energy and focus are now different.

If you were focusing on your spouse and his or her needs more than on yourself, you may feel even more adrift and fragmented. What do you do about all you used to do is a dilemma. It may be difficult for you to take the step that's necessary at this time—focusing on and taking care of you. And it's not only about who you are now; it also includes who you want to be in the future.

You may not feel there is a future, but there will be, and you have a hand in shaping it. At this point in time, it may be overwhelming just to get through the day, let alone consider next month or next year. But at some point, you will. And as you do, enlist the help of others who are wise, compassionate and supportive to assist you. Just as you don't want to grieve in isolation, it is best to enlist others in planning for your future. The wisdom and knowledge found in Scripture can help you grasp the hope of a future:

> "For I know the plans I have for you," declares the LORD, "plans to prosper you and not to harm you, plans to give you hope and a future" (Jer. 29:11).

> Call to me [the Lord] and I will answer you and tell you great and

unsearchable things you do not know (Jer. 33:3).

You won't be the same person three months, six months or a year or two from now. And you don't move forward *when* the grief is concluded, but *while* it is present. Some of us will go in and out of grief for years, even when we've built an entirely new life. That is normal. What you do with your time, energy, resources, heart and mind will be different. (And if you could foresee the future, you would probably be surprised at how active and involved your life will become.)

In Search of Your New Identity

The death of your spouse created an abrupt change in your identity, much of which was defined by your marriage. The death of that relationship frequently shatters your world in a different way.

Two questions are important here: *Who am I?* and *Who do I want to become?* The search for and development of a new identity is a large part of moving forward in your life.

In the space below, describe your identity at three separate points: past, present and future. Reflect on your responses. Write down as much detail as possible and keep doing this for a while.[4]

Who was I?

_____
_____

Who am I?

_____
_____

Who do I want to become?

_____
_____

Feelings. You're probably overwhelmed by feelings. They're terrible—out of control and like a category-5 hurricane. There is no sense or reason to them. These are common and painful cries expressed by many. People have said that grief is the blackest night of confusion because of all the emotions. Your range of feelings is like a smorgasbord. Each day you have a wide variety to choose from.

There will also be daily variations that come and go. You may think some emotions are gone for good—but not so. They disappear, reappear and overlap. Thankfully, over time, they will become less frequent and less intense.

Gay Hendricks provides this innovative way to look at feelings:

> Think of a painful feeling as being like a bonfire in a field. At first it is hot, unapproachable. Later it may still smolder. Even later, you can walk on the ground without pain, but you know there is an essence of the fire that still remains. Take your own time, but be sure to walk over the ground again. You must do so because whatever you run away from runs you.[5]

As we discussed in chapter 1, the feelings hit when you least expect them.

Some of these most common feelings and concerns may or may not describe you at this particular time:

- *"I feel like I've lost my best friend."*
  And for some, they have. Marriage holds the greatest potential for intimacy of any relationship. Now

the shared experiences have ceased and the comfort of knowing another so well, along with an abundance of automatic responses, is gone.

- *"I feel angry."* To whom or to what is your anger directed? At yourself, the doctors, the hospital, your spouse, at God? Anger is a feeling of displeasure, irritation and protest. In grief, especially, it is a protest, a desire to make someone pay, to declare the unfairness of the death. You're feeling frustrated, hurt, afraid and helpless. Sometimes anger is expressed like a missile. It erupts suddenly from the silo. There's no warning. And there is damage. Another day your anger may be expressed in silent withdrawal. It's subtle, but it's still there. And sometimes the anger is frozen. It's solid and heavy. You can start to deal with it by identifying at what or at whom your anger is directed. Write it out. Draw it. Tell a trusted friend. Write a letter and read it out loud.

It may be especially hard to admit that you are angry toward God. Your anger may be directed at Him for not responding in the way you wanted when your spouse was sick or injured. Or maybe it's because your faith and beliefs didn't seem to work, since healing didn't occur. The distress you feel over the failure of God to respond in the way you needed Him to can prolong your grief. Tell God your feelings. He can handle it.

Loss and fear go hand in hand. We can be afraid of how we'll survive being alone now and forever; afraid of driving, of sounds in the night, of finances, of the reactions of others, and so on.

You may be a person for whom fear has never found a residence before now. But now it has moved in. Fear can disable you by crippling your relationships with others and making life more of a chore than it actually is. Fear leads you to imagine the worst, and this leads to anxiety and dread. As Hendricks states:

> Fear can be debilitating. Some people experience fear in a small number of areas, while others are overwhelmed by it. It is perfectly natural to be fearful. We have

experienced the most unexpected tragedy. Common fears include: fearing any situation that remotely resembles how the loved one died, fearing that others we love will be harmed, fearing we will not be able to go on, fearing we will die ourselves, and fearing the simplest activities will lead to tragedy.[6]

In the space below, write out some of your current fears and what you can do to face those fears.[7]

1. I am afraid of...

_____

_____

What can I do about it?

_____

_____

2. I am afraid of...

_____

_____

What can I do about it?

_____

_____

3. I am afraid of...

_____

_____

_____

What can I do about it?

_____

_____

_____

4.   What other fears do I have?

_____

_____

_____

Isolation can take hold of your life and assume several forms. In the extreme, we sit in our homes with the shades drawn, the lights down low, seeing no one and venturing outside only when absolutely necessary. We believe that our pain is so great that we can't possibly relate to or interact with anyone, so we basically lock ourselves away from the rest of the world.

Another form of isolation occurs when you have a desire for interaction but you're uncertain how to proceed. You wait for someone to issue a dinner invitation or offer to go shopping or attend a social event, and when those invitations don't come, you think your

friends have forgotten about you. Two conditions bring this on:
1. Friends—most of whom have never experienced what you are going through—don't understand your needs or how they can help.
2. In many cases, when asked, "How are you doing?" or when help is offered, you respond with comments such as, "I'm doing as well as I can expect" or "I can't think of anything."

Such support is generally received in a very narrow scope, such as at work or church, not necessarily when needed the most. It's not because no one wants to help but because they don't know what or when to give. The key is to tell people what you want or need.

Isolation is one of the most dangerous traps; it is a leading cause of depression among surviving spouses. You can best avoid isolation through involvement in activities at work, in your community and at church.[8]

Have you been in the hospital for an operation? If so, you know that after the operation is over, you're taken to a recovery room where you stay for a few hours until the effects of the anesthesia wear off. The term "recovery room" is a bit misleading. It certainly doesn't mean total recovery. It means making sure you've adjusted to the effects of the operation so that you're ready for the healing and a healthier you. It's the same with grief. "Recovery" doesn't mean getting back to the way you were before. That won't happen. You have to develop a new life, a new normal. Recovery is actually relearning your life.

During the early months of grief, relearning is like having to get off the main highway every so many miles because the direct route is under construction. The road signs route you through a little town you hadn't expected to visit and over bumpy roads you weren't planning on bouncing over. You're basically traveling in the appropriate direction. On a map, however, the course you're following would have the look of sharks' teeth instead of a straight line. Although you are gradually getting where you want to be, you sometimes doubt you'll ever meet up with the finished highway.

Haven't you felt this way? I have—and my friends have.

How do you develop a new way of relating to the one you lost? Death ends the person's life but not your relationship. This isn't morbid or pathological. It's perfectly normal. But few talk about it. Have you heard a discussion about such a relationship as being normal? Probably not. If you bring it up for discussion, people might worry that you've gone over the edge. If people tell you that the best way to deal with your loss is to forget the person or not think about him or her, they're blocking your grief experience. Don't listen to them.

We keep people alive all the time. We reflect on who they were, what their achievements were and how they impacted society. I've heard a number of people make the statements, "I wonder what he would think if he were alive today?" or "Wouldn't she be surprised to see all of this?" People contemplate what their deceased spouse would do in certain situations, using memories of what the person would do as one of several options.

What is abnormal is if you feel you must do things or see things just the way your spouse did. You don't. You have a choice.

Recovery, or relearning, does not mean a once-and-for-all conclusion to your loss and grief. It is a twofold process that involves regaining the ability to function as you once did and resolving and making sense of your loss. But there is something else to recovery.

Recovery means feeling better. Recovery means claiming your circumstances instead of letting your circumstances claim your happiness. Recovery is finding new meaning for living without the fear of future abandonment. Recovery is being able to enjoy fond memories without having them precipitate painful feelings of loss, guilt, regret or remorse. Recovery is acknowledging that it is perfectly all right to feel bad from time to time and to talk about those feelings no matter how those around you react. Recovery is being able to forgive others when they say or do things that you know are based on their lack of knowledge about grief. Recovery is one day realizing that your ability to talk about the loss you've experienced is, in fact, helping another person get through his or her grief.

Recovery means reinvesting in life by looking for new relationships and new dreams. It is possible to find a new source of joy. You may feel odd though. You could very well feel uncomfortable with whatever is new. You may feel that to experience joy again is somehow wrong. And there's the fear that if you begin to hope again or trust again, you could experience another loss.

Remember who is the *source* of joy. It is the Lord. The psalmist states that God "clothes us with joy" (see Ps. 30:11). He is the one who extends to us the invitation to reinvest in life.

Grief recovery is a back-and-forth process. One of the better ways to identify your progress is through writing in a personal journal. This will provide proof that you are making progress even when your feelings say otherwise. Your journal is your *private* property and is *not* for anyone else to read. It's an expression of what you are feeling right now in your recovery. It can be written in any style, but it's best done longhand so that your thoughts flow and you can add art, drawings and illustrations as you feel like it. You can also put in simple statements, poems and prayers that reflect your journey.

If you'd like help getting started on a personal journal, here are some questions you can ask and answer:
- What do I miss most about my spouse?
- What do I wish I had asked or said to my spouse?
- What do I wish I had done or not done?
- What do I wish my spouse had said or not said?
- What do I wish my spouse had done or not done?
- What did I value most about our relationship?
- What was hurtful or angering about our relationship?
- What special moments do I remember about my spouse?
- What memories will I keep alive?

- What will I keep to cherish as a part of my spouse and our relationship?
- What living situation is difficult for me to deal with without my spouse?[9]

If you need to say goodbye, what can you do? Many have found it helpful to write a goodbye or farewell letter. This may be an emotional experience for you, but it can bring you a sense of completeness. That's the purpose of your letter—to *complete* your relationship. You may believe that it already was complete, and yet as you reflect upon it, you may realize that there were things you wish you'd said or done or wish your spouse had said or done. You're not alone in feeling like this.

It's good to be aware of how your relationship was incomplete. Accept the responsibility for your role in its being incomplete, and then contemplate what wasn't said that needs to be said.[10]

Remember that no marriage is perfect. It's in a constant process of growth. A marriage doesn't demand perfection; what is needed is priority. As one friend said, "It's an institution for sinners, and no one else need apply. And it finds its finest glory when we sinners see it as God's way of leading us through his ultimate curriculum of love and righteousness."

Some people lose their partners at a time when their marriage was rich and fulfilling. Others lose their spouse when their union was troubled and distant. No matter what the state the marriage was in, death hurts.

Necessary Steps Forward

There are some steps you can take to move on after the death of your loved one. The first step is simple: Make amends. Making amends is not just saying you're sorry for what you regret; it's also about changing your responses. Ask, "What positive or negative events or situations did I not make amends for?" You can be sorry for something you did or for something you wished you'd done or said. Here are some additional suggestions:

- *Identify what doesn't make sense to you about the loss of your spouse.* Perhaps there's a vague question

about life or God's purpose for you. Or it could be a specific question: "Why did this have to happen to me now, at this crucial point in my life?"
- *Identify the emotions you feel during each day.*
- *State the steps or actions you are taking to help you move ahead.* Identify what you have done in the past that has helped. Ask a trusted friend for help.
- *Share your loss and grief with others who will listen to you and support you.* Don't seek advice givers, but do find those friends who are empathetic and can handle your feelings.
- *Find a person who has experienced a similar loss.* Groups and organizations abound for losses of all types.
- *Identify the positive characteristics and struggles of your life that helped you before.*
- *Spend time reading in the book of Psalms.*
- *Share your confusion, your feelings and your hopes with God.* Even if

you're angry with God, sharing your protest is an act of faith and belief.
- *Think about where you want to be two years from now.* Write out some of your dreams and goals.
- *Become familiar with the process of grief.* Knowing what to expect helps you to not get thrown by what you're experiencing or will experience.
- *Remember that understanding your grief intellectually isn't enough.* It can't replace the emotional experience of living through this difficult time.

Is recalling how a loved one died necessary? Is it normal? The answer to both questions is yes. Repetitious reviewing helps you fully realize that your needs, hopes, expectations and dreams of continuing to be with this person are *not* going to be fulfilled. You simply can't be with your spouse the way you used to be. Each time you review the death and surrounding events, your understanding of this will increase, and perhaps more meaning will be added. You may tend to resist reflection since the memories bring pain; but each time you remember, you'll discover you have more control.[11]

What are the healthy ways to handle the fact that your spouse is dead and yet keep him or her alive in memory for you and others? This may sound strange, but the initial step is recognizing that the person is *gone* and *you* are still alive. At first you may not feel as though you're very much alive. Sometimes people say they can't go on or don't want to go on without their spouse. But there does need to come a time of emotionally letting go and reinvesting in life in a new way.

Another step is deciding what there is about your life with the other person and your life together that can and should be restructured. This includes deciding what is healthy.

What would your spouse want for you?

Letting go completely of the past, and then moving into and embracing living again, is one of the most difficult steps you must take because you might believe that experiencing happiness and joy might somehow reflect disrespect to the memory of your deceased wife or husband. Deep down, you know what she or he would want for you as you move forward.

So focus on the following three questions. Your answers can open your eyes to a clear path toward living again.

1. What would your spouse want for you?

_____
_____

2. How will you make this a reality?

_____
_____

3. Would achieving this improve life as you know it today? How, specifically?[12]

_____
_____

Perhaps the words reflecting the journey of this husband can help you in yours. He wrote this in the second year following the death of his wife, and he has given me permission to share it with you.

I suppose I was not much different from most men when it

came to dealing with death, whether it was my own death or that of a loved one. I would not allow myself to fully contemplate my own death, and most certainly not that of my wife, Susan, whom I loved and was devoted to for more than 20 years. Yet, in the span of three short months, Susan died from complications associated with breast cancer.

To say that I was unprepared for her sudden death would be a gross understatement. I was totally and completely caught off guard, mentally and spiritually. As a result, I was thrown into a mental and physical tailspin of denial and disbelief, a denial that manifested in an overwhelming sense of guilt and depression and a state of mourning that was beyond psychological comprehension.

I suddenly found myself trying to deal with a situation that just a few days before was beyond the scope of my daily life, much less a soon-to-be reality. I found myself grasping for reasons why this would happen to Susan, how it could happen so suddenly and what was to happen to me. Without warning the ebb and flow of what was once a normal and happy life had drastically changed for the worst. All that I knew and loved had not only changed but was lost forever. A wave of deep depression and extreme selfishness washed over my soul with the loss of Susan.

I had what I considered a perfect marriage relationship. I was a kept man in every sense of the word. That is to say, whatever my need, Susan willingly and happily met that need. Whether it was sexually, socially, physically or spiritually, she was there. Susan was not just my wife; she was my best friend, closest confidant and a voice of sound reason when I was unreasonable. I suddenly found myself having to deal with life in all of its fullness, feeling both alone and abandoned. I felt as if I was on an island of humanity, isolated within myself, void of family and friends. For the first time in my married life, I had no answers for what lay before me or what I was about to endure. I found myself an unwilling participant in a mental endurance run with no end in sight. All I knew was that I needed help to navigate this run, and I needed it now.

Isolated, depressed and feeling sorry for myself, I realized I needed help that was beyond my spiritual, physical and mental abilities. So I turned to the roots of my raising—a raising that required a rededication of my life to church and, most importantly, a closer walk with Jesus. Yet, I was conflicted on the best way to accomplish this; for after all, in recent years, I was not actively participating in church. This made me feel somewhat guilty asking my church for help, but I was willing to do anything and seek any advice if it would ease my pain, isolation and depression. As it happened, my pastor informed me of a class that was being conducted by another local church, called GriefShare.

Unable to function in daily life, I found myself operating on autopilot. However, I was able to pull myself together enough to contact the church conducting the GriefShare class and make arrangements to attend the next available classes. As it turned out, attending the GriefShare class was one of the best decisions I made in the early stages of my grief and mourning. I found that the class, while informal, was as its name implied: shared grief. It was not a course in which, after a class or two, you would be apathetic. The class was not designed for that; however, it was a class that brought together others who were grieving as deeply as I was, although for different reasons, while creating a common bond. Additionally, it provided me with an outlet and a facility to freely express my feelings with others who were enduring similar circumstances of grief and mourning.

In the early stages of the class, I noticed that a phrase kept popping up throughout the 13-week course. As I attended more classes, I came to cringe at its utterance. The phrase was "starting a new normal." I didn't know what it meant, nor could anyone fully explain or define what that phrase was supposed to mean. As it turned out, the phrase had a different meaning for each person. My challenge was to discover what my "new normal" was to be.

While I truly can't say that I have discovered its complete meaning as it applies to me, I do believe that I'm beginning to understand its meaning a little better. As I take stock of my life, as it is now, I realize that my life is a circle from sunrise to sundown. As long as it continues in this manner, I know that I will always have a new day dawning. I believe that eventually my circled life of sunrise to sundown will straighten into a path laden with peril but also a new beginning. When that day comes, then I'll be able to say that

I do have a "new normal" that begins today.

The New International Version of the Bible states in Ecclesiastes 7:2, "It is better to go to a house of mourning than to go to a house of feasting, for death is the destiny of every man." I found this passage while searching for some divine or profound meaning to my life as it is now. As I dwelt on its concept, I did struggle with its meaning as I understood it. While death is the destiny of every man, it is inescapable, just as mourning is. However, the house of feasting is just a temporary condition. The feeling of euphoria, while wondrous, is short-lived and provides little comfort or spiritual assistance. The house of mourning, on the other hand, is a time-tested tempering of your soul and spirit, and faith that your prayers will be answered. Mourning, however painful, is God's way to test your faith, and the trying of your faith by divine fires. Once completed, you will have faith that you will stand the test of time and your devotion to God's plan for you.

Through these past few months, I prayed many prayers and there were many prayers prayed on my behalf by family and friends. However, none of them seemed to have reached the ear of God. Then, one day when I was in my hour of deepest depression and isolation, I began to pray a very simple prayer.

Lord, You know my needs. All I ask is that You provide a single healing stitch to my heart once a day. I know that over time, while the scar in my heart will always remain, the healing can begin.

I find that I miss Susan more than I can say, and I will forever love her. I know that the healing process of my heart has begun, however gradually, for God does answer prayer if you only have faith.[13]

Recommended Resources

H. Norman Wright, *Reflections of a Grieving Spouse: The Unexpected*

Journey from Loss to Renewed Hope (Eugene, OR: Harvest House, 2009).

    I highly recommend your participation in a GriefShare group. Go to www.griefshare.org to learn of one near you.

3

The Death of a Child

Our son died. That's all we could say. Matthew died. It shouldn't have happened. Parents are not supposed to outlive their children.

Matthew was 22 when he died on March 15, the Ides of March. His life and ours had been full of losses, for he was born with brain damage and was profoundly mentally disabled. Mentally, his development was that of an 18-month-old and he had just a few words to say. He also had some physical impairment. He lived with us for 11 years, and then he lived at Salem Christian Home for his last 11 years. He came home at least once a month for the weekend. Matthew, whose name means "gift from God," was indeed that, for he changed our lives both in his life and in his death.

Matthew's impact came not so much from what he said, for that was very limited. It was not so much from what he did, for that, too, was very limited.

In fact, that's the word that best describes him—*limited*—but perhaps only in the ways that we think are the most significant. His calling was to teach and refine those around him, and that he did, even though he wasn't aware of it because his limitations got in the way.

His limitations were actually what made him so effective. Had he been what the world calls normal, our lives as parents would have been less painful but so much more ordinary. God used him to make the truth of Scripture more alive, more real and more relevant to us. He used Matthew to teach us to reevaluate our values, to modify our expectations, to appreciate aspects of life taken for granted, to become more fully human, and to learn to grow more dependent upon God.

Matthew died after corrective surgery for reflux esophagitis. And we began a never-ending journey of being the parents of a child who was no longer with us. If you're reading this chapter, you're probably there as well and wondering, *Where do I go with the rest of my life?*

The Ultimate Bereavement

The death of a child is unlike any other loss. It's a horrendous shock, no matter how it happens. But you already know that.

One of the most difficult and disturbing issues to handle is the wrongness of a child's death. It just shouldn't happen. It doesn't make sense. It's death out of turn. Parents ask themselves, *Why should I survive when our child, who should have survived, didn't?* Death violates the cycle that children grow up and replace the old.

When you lose a child, your world turns upside down. And it's not just your world that is destroyed. It impacts so many others, including grandparents, aunts, uncles, cousins, friends, and so on. But if you are grieving parents, your grief is the most complex and intense; unless the others in your life have lost a child, they won't fully understand. It's as if you have been forced through a crack in your world where your beliefs and expectations have been turned inside out. As authors Mary Ann and James Emswiler state:

> Bereaved parents often say, "It's not right!" "It doesn't compute!"—and these bizarre, unreal, and not-right feelings spread to other parts of their life. This means that the ripples of this horror not only flow inward, affecting one's sense of self, but also outward—to your marriage, the deceased child's siblings, as well as to extended family and friends. The waves of grief also flow out to school friends and teachers, health care providers, neighbors, workplace peers, the faith community, the people from whom you buy food and services, mail delivery people, and anyone else who has regular contact with you. All are affected and nothing will ever be the same again in any of the social systems connected with your family.[1]

Years ago, when infectious diseases ran wild, death in children was common. That has changed, and most deaths occur naturally and expectedly among the elderly. Our society is prepared for death with this group and handles it relatively well. But the thought-to-be-infrequent occurrence of child death is more traumatic.

When you lose a child, you also lose what your child represented to you. You feel victimized in so many ways. You feel as though you've lost part of yourself, or even part of your physical body. Those features in the child that bore resemblance to you or your spouse hit the hardest.

You will miss the physical interaction as well—the sight, sound, smell and touch of your child. If you were still in the hands-on, caregiving stage with your child, this absence will be terribly painful.

Your child embodied your connection to the future, too, and that no longer exists. If your child was old enough to respond to you, you've lost a very special love source. That love was based on need, dependence, admiration and appreciation, but now it's gone. You've lost some of your own treasured qualities and talents as well, for you saw some of those that you value most in your child. Further, you've lost the expectations and dreams you had for your child when he or she grew older. The anticipated years, full of so many special events, were ripped away from you. You experience so many other losses as well.

Losing Matthew was a tremendous blow in and of itself. But like any other major loss, it also caused a number of additional, or secondary, losses. The routine we had followed for years was gone forever. We would no longer look through catalogs to select his special sleepwear. We wouldn't have the special weekends in which he would come home and stay overnight, nor would we be able to stop by Salem Home to take him out to eat. Instead, we would drive past where he used to live and keep traveling along the freeway.

We faced future losses as well. Matthew would no longer be at home for Thanksgiving or Christmas; we wouldn't take him to Knott's Berry Farm for his birthday. Those losses we could anticipate, but each week brought others that we didn't expect. (If he had been living at home, there would have been daily losses.) We couldn't call

Salem House anymore to see how he was doing; a topic of our conversation was gone; certain phrases or expressions we would say to him would no longer be expressed.

Sometimes the way we discovered the other losses was surprising. Eight months after Matthew died, we acquired a new dog. For years we had raised shelties, but now we selected a golden retriever puppy that we named Sheffield. One day, when I walked by the kitchen and through the door, I heard Joyce saying something to Sheffield that stopped me in my tracks. I opened the door and said, "What did you just say to Sheff?"

She said, "Oh, I was just saying, 'Hey you,' while I was playing with him."

Then it dawned on her, as it had on me, that she had frequently used that expression when talking to Matthew. We hadn't heard it for such a long time, and we felt his loss again.

Another day, we took the dog to the vet for shots and a checkup. my wife wrapped Sheffield in a large towel and held him on her lap as we drove.

Halfway there, she began crying, and I looked over and asked what was wrong. "I just realized this is the same towel I always used with Matthew when I bathed him at home and that I wouldn't be using this on him anymore," she said. "I want to save this towel and remember the happy bubble baths." Once again, we felt the intrusion of a loss.

You may also see your child's death as a failure on your part. You feel anger and frustration for being unable to exert some control over what happened to your child.[2]

One counselor graphically describes this feeling:

> In this way, losing your child means losing parts of yourself. One bereaved mother described it this way: "When you lose your spouse, it is like losing a limb, when you lose your child, it is like losing your lung." Not only does this happen because of the emotional investment you have in your child and the needs, hopes and dreams you have for her; it also happens because parental attachment to a child

consists of both love for the child and self-love.

With the death of your child you have failed in the basic function of parenthood: taking care of the children and the family. You are supposed to protect and provide for your child. You are supposed to keep her from all harm. She should be the one who grows up healthy to bury you.

When you "fail" at this, when your child dies, you may feel that you have failed at your most basic function.

The death of any child is a monumental assault on your sense of identity. Because you cannot carry out your role of preserving your child, you may experience an oppressive sense of failure, a loss of power and ability, and a deep sense of being violated. Disillusionment, emptiness, and insecurity may follow, all of which stem from a diminished sense of self. And this can lead to the guilt that is such a common feature in parental grief.[3]

Parental guilt can take many forms. Some parents experience survival guilt, the feeling that it's not right that they're still alive and their child isn't. There can also be illness-related guilt, where the parent thinks some personal deficiency caused the child's sickness and death. Some parents experience guilt over the belief that in some unknown way they either contributed to their child's death or failed to protect the child. And some experience moral guilt over the belief that the child's death was punishment for *their* violation of some moral or religious code.[4] As Dan Schaefer and Christine Lyons write in *How Do We Tell the Children:*

> In those situations where the death results from genetic or unexplained medical factors, parents often take on additional burdens of grief. They try to explain why their child died prematurely and violated the laws of nature. Parents hold themselves responsible for not producing a healthy child that could survive longer, and often feel deficient and worthless as a result. Often, when answers about the

cause of death are not forthcoming, parents tend to search all the way back to the earliest prenatal expectation: "Perhaps it was because I took the aspirin when I was pregnant that she developed the beginnings of the illness that took her life at 11."[5]

Because of all these losses, your grief over the death of a child will be more intense and last longer than grief over the loss of anyone else. The death of a child has been called the ultimate bereavement. You need to accept this and let others know about it as well. Perhaps you can relate to what this parent said:

> My child has died, and I'm faced with what seems inconceivable—life without my child. I have been forced to embark on a journey that is so different than any I have taken before. Nothing could have prepared me for this loss or for the intensity of the grief that I feel. It's so painful. The death of a child is like no other. My life has been totally shattered; I will never again be the person I was before my

child's death. Life is different. I'm different. Days stretch endlessly; they're filled with a pain that is deeper than any I've ever before felt. My heart feels like it's been pierced. A part of me has died. Will I always feel the overwhelming emptiness? Will I ever again experience a sense of wholeness? Does life have meaning if my son is no longer here to share it with me? Does it?[6]

You'll continually struggle with anger—anger at what happened, at anyone you feel could have prevented it, at the unfairness of what transpired, at the disruption of your life, and at God. The anger will come and go for years.

As a bereaved parent, you'll have to "grow up with the loss." Parents tend to mark their lives by the events involving and the accomplishments of their children. The dates when those events would have occurred will still come around, even though your child won't be there to experience them. The sixth birthday; the first teen birthday; the times when your child would have received a driver's license, graduated, married and had children; all will bring a resurgence of your grief when you least expect it.

When your child dies because of a terminal disease, you get a double dose of grief. Before your child's death, you grieve over the fact that your child is going to die. Afterward, you grieve the actual death. Even though you know it's going to occur and you've known that for weeks, months or years, it's still devastating. We used to hear about this situation mostly with parents whose children had cancer, but more and more we hear it about children dying of AIDS.

The trauma of coping with a terminally ill child redefines your entire life. Perhaps you've never experienced it yourself, but we're called to be compassionate and supportive of others. Knowing what other parents face may speak to your heart. When a child is dying, it's as though the future is canceled for a time. The entire focus is on the present. Priorities change and future plans and dreams are jeopardized. If the future is considered at all, it is with dread. Listen to the words of fathers and mothers who lost a child after a long illness:

- A mother whose 17-year-old son died of bone cancer: "There was no future for us. We were afraid of what tomorrow and the next day might bring. We learned to savor every good moment, every good day. We didn't allow ourselves to even think beyond that day. The future was a frightening place for us."
- A mother whose eight-year-old son died of leukemia: "You concentrate on the good days and live for those. You have to grasp them as they come. You have to take the bad days too, but you want to get them over quickly. When you have a good day, you want it to last forever. You never want to let it go."
- A father whose four-year-old son died of leukemia: "We had to readjust our whole life when Sam became ill. All our future plans had to be shelved. I didn't even want to think about the future because I knew it held Sam's death. It was just too unbearable to think about."

- A mother whose six-year-old daughter died of leukemia: "Her death was not imminent to me. This was something in the future; it was far away. I lived only for today. I didn't even think about tomorrow, let alone plan for it."[7]

When your child is diagnosed as terminally ill, it may take days for reality to sink in. As one parent said, "I think nature prepares you for these times. You can only absorb a small amount of information at one time. You hear the words but they don't sink in. The true reality comes to you over a span of time—a little at a time. I know it was several hours before I was able to grasp the full weight of what was said to me, and several days for the emotional impact to ripple through me."

A mother of a terminally ill child named Mark said the following:

> We took Mark to a specialist who put him in the hospital for surgery the next day. We were confident of the outcome. I think I developed an optimism that supported me at that time. I went to the hospital alone with Mark and

was waiting in the reception area when they called me into the hall. The doctor was standing there with his hands in his surgical gloves raised in front of him just like you see on TV. He had come out of surgery halfway through to talk with me. All he said was "I've got some bad news—it's cancer!" I just stood there. I don't think I ever in my life experienced that kind of feeling of shock! No preparation! Everything stopped! It was as if I stuck to the floor! I couldn't move! I couldn't speak! I knew that hospital well but I couldn't even think what floor Mark's room was on. I walked up and down the corridors aimlessly. Those ugly words—"it's cancer"—were repeated over and over in my mind. I tried to call home but I couldn't even remember my own phone number![8]

If you were the parent of a terminally ill child, you probably experienced one or more of the following common reactions: You may not have accepted the diagnosis and prognosis when they were initially revealed to you. (This also happens when you're told your child has a disability.) You assimilate the diagnosis and prognosis gradually or deny them right up to the last moments with your child.

Perhaps you fantasized consciously or subconsciously about a miraculous recovery for your child.

You may have tried to bring about a healing yourself through arranging for a healing service, having the elders of the church pray and anoint your child with oil, providing a special diet, going for a special treatment banned in this country, using visualization techniques, or bargaining with God.

You may have felt your child's illness was some form of punishment for something you did in the past or even thought about.[9]

When Grief Support Is Minimal or Nonexistent

One of the struggles of moving through grief when you've lost a child is when your support is minimal or non-existent. Not only may others avoid you, but they may also shun your grief. Isolation feels terribly painful. You feel like an invisible griever. In some ways the loss of a child involves a "death" of the parent.

There are also several types of deaths for which a parent receives minimal help. One is when your child is murdered. This death is so public. Your child becomes part of the hunt for the killer and the trial, and this can continue for years. Friends and others aren't sure how to respond to you.

Suicide creates guilt, for as a parent, you feel this was a death you could have stopped. Others aren't sure how to respond, and many parents often withdraw and shut themselves off from the support they need. (An excellent book for this circumstance is *Finding Your Way After the Suicide of Someone You Love,* by David B. Biebel and Suzanne L. Foster.)

A missing child, such as a runaway or a child who has been kidnapped, puts grief on hold for years. At first it is a struggle to accept that the child is missing. Most support is related to helping in the search rather than in grieving. The grief pattern is intensified and delayed.

If your child was in the armed services and is missing in action (MIA), you probably have to share your limited support with his or her spouse and children. It's difficult to grieve with no solution to his or her whereabouts. There is no closure.

If you're new in town, it's difficult to get a support system, and you may feel isolated.

One of the other child losses quickly forgotten is miscarriage. Insensitive comments abound. Few people realize that it usually takes 6 to 10 months to recover emotionally with this loss.

And then there is abortion. It is the loss of a child. But like miscarriage, few see it as a source of grief. There is little support, and often the mother doesn't share the experience or reach out for help. Comfort from other people is lacking.

A mother who gives her child up for adoption rarely receives support for her loss. The adoptive mother becomes the focus of joy and excitement, which can add to the pain of the birth mother. Usually there's little support for her.

There are many variations of experience regarding the loss of a child.[10]

Grandparents—The Forgotten Grievers

After the death of a child, there can be a number of invisible or forgotten grievers, including grandparents. They experience what is known as a dual loss. They grieve for their grandchild as well as for their adult child's suffering. Grandparents are neglected since the death of a grandchild is a generation removed. But often grandparents have hopes and dreams invested in their grandchild, and when a death occurs, like parents they feel like they have lost a part of themselves. A grandchild often represents a grandparent's immortality, and when death occurs, there's a sense of devastation.

The grandparent-grandchild relationship is like no other. For many, the arrival of a grandchild is like "reliving spring in the autumn of your life."[11]

Grandparents live with constant losses, such as health, finances, change of residence, and death of family and friends. The presence of a grandchild can be the bright spot in a grandparent's life. Time spent together is special since the day-to-day responsibilities and conflicts are limited or nonexistent.[12]

Often grandparents experience the deep agony of seeing the pain of their own grieving child and want to help, but they aren't always certain of what to do or say. They may end up having to parent their own child again, which could be difficult. As the author of *Grandparents Cry Twice* said:

> Grandparents cannot protect their child from, nor take away, the child's pain. Extreme effort is required to be available and helpful to their adult child and his/her family all the while watching their suffering. This puts an extraordinary demand on grandparents' love, understanding, knowledge, and abilities—not to mention stamina.

The extraordinary emotional and psychological effort grandparents experience trying to cope with a grandchild's death often seems to be a challenge far beyond what most grandparents believe they can endure. No one ever expects to have to fill this particular role in life and there aren't any training manuals![13]

You may be overwhelmed with your own grief. Ask others to reach out to your parents, as well as to your deceased child's siblings. No one should be forgotten.[14]

No matter how you lose a child, the questions arise: "How do I recover?" "What steps can I take to survive?" We've looked at loss and grief in an overall manner, but let's consider other aspects now.

How Child Loss Affects a Marriage

Following the death of a child, a marriage may tend to flounder. It's as though the very structure of your family life is under attack. You may have to intervene with your other children as they react to the loss of their brother or sister. You and your spouse may struggle with vocational pressures because of being distracted and absent from your job for an extended period. Daily routines seem overwhelming because of your grief, and you may pick at each other when you see things left undone. There could be a new financial burden because of the child's illness or the unbelievably high expense of a funeral. All these elements add to marital tension.

It is estimated that 90 percent of all couples who lose a child face some kind of marital struggle within the first year after the death. The divorce rate is high among couples who have lost an only child.[15] Statistics also show that in approximately 70 percent of the families where a child was killed violently, parents either separated or divorced.[16] Many marriages that dissolve were held together only by a slim thread to begin with, and this event seemed to snap the remaining strand. It could also be that the parenting roles were more intense than the marital relationship.

The death of a child, however, does not have to lead to divorce. It can become a time of mutual comfort, support and growth.

No parent is ever prepared to lose a child, regardless of the cause or the child's age. But you can *learn* to recover and survive, and it is a learning process. There are no shortcuts to your grieving. It's painful and long, and you will wish it would go away. You're living in a dark tunnel, and you're not sure there's any light at the end. But when you keep searching for the light, you will find it. This grief lingers longer than any other, and you carry the remnants of shadow grief for years.

Ronald Knapp gives us this insightful description of shadow grief:

> Shadow grief reveals itself more in the form of an emotional "dullness," where the person is unable to respond fully and completely to outer stimulation and where normal activity is moderately inhibited. It is characterized as a dull ache in the background of one's

feelings that remains fairly constant and that, under certain circumstances and on certain occasions, comes bubbling to the surface, sometimes in the form of tears, sometimes not, but always accompanied by a feeling of sadness and a mild sense of anxiety. Shadow grief will vary in intensity depending on the person and the unique factors involved. It is more emotional for some than for others.

Where shadow grief exists, the individual can never remember the events surrounding the loss without feeling some kind of emotional reaction, regardless of how mild.

The difference between "normal" grief and "shadow" grief is similar to the difference between pneumonia and the common cold. The latter is less serious, less disruptive to life, more of a nuisance than anything else.[17]

I, too, carry this shadow grief, even though it's been more than 20 years since Matthew died. When it hits, I say, "This is normal, and I needed to cry again."

No one can tell you how long this grief will last. Grief has a beginning, a middle and an end. But many parents get stuck in the middle, and most don't understand the dynamics and duration of grief, which makes it even more difficult to adjust.

Most of us don't realize there's a pattern of peaks and valleys in grief. Look at the intensity of grief as indicated by this chart:

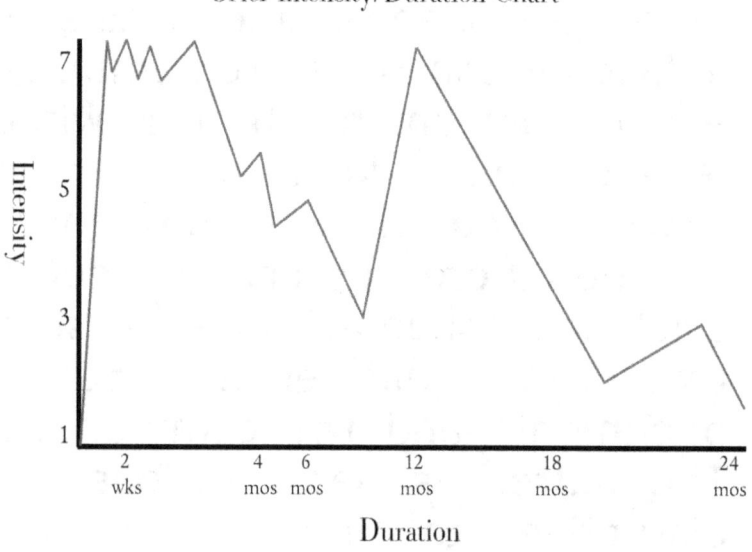

Notice the jagged peaks. The pain and grief actually intensify at three months and then gradually subside, but not steadily. They go up and down. Most people don't need a reminder of the first-year anniversary of the loss of a loved one. The grief comes rushing in with pain that rivals the initial feelings. If anyone tries to tell you that you should be over it by now, or feeling better, at any of the peak times, you may become quite upset. That's understandable. It's also understandable that people don't appreciate the grief process unless they've been through it themselves.[18]

By now you've probably been wounded by the remarks of others. If not, you will be. These are people from whom you will never get the support you need and want from them. You will struggle with what others say. You will get tired of responding to "How are you feeling?" Some grieving parents carry the little book *Experiencing Grief* with them. When asked, they say, "Thank you for asking. This little book describes what I'm going through." By doing this, you take some pressure off of yourself as well as help them prepare for a loss in their future.

Here are other responses:
- "You can help me most by just listening to me for a while."

- "Advice is not what I need right now."
- "I don't want to talk right now. I hope you understand."
- "That comment was not only unhelpful, it hurt me."
- "Can you just sit with me while I cry for a little while?"[19]

If you have lost a child, you may want to give this section of the book or the "Grief Intensity/Duration Chart" to those around you to help them understand. You could also make a copy of "The Crazy Feelings of Grief" in chapter 1 to give to others to make them aware of your journey. Or ask your minister to explain these facts to your congregation.

The usual time for recovering from the loss of a loved one in a normal loss is two years. But throw away that measure when dealing with the loss of a child; it will be longer, much longer. With many parents, it can take from 6 to 10 years to stabilize. Most of us think if we can survive the first year, the following years will be better.

The author of *When Your Child Dies* wrote:

But a number of bereaved parents cite periods in the second or third year after their child dies as being even more painful than the first year. It was during these times when parents emerged into the profound realization that their son or daughter was dead and would never be coming back. As difficult as this deeper realization is to experience, however, you will—in a way—be in a better position to engage with it. You have lived with your grief and survived what you once believed to be unbearable.

You cannot change the fact that your child has died. You can, however, decide how you will live a life that not only honors the memory of your child, but one that again holds meaning and purpose.[20]

Your tears will come for years. Let them. One morning they hit me in our worship service at Hollywood Presbyterian Church. The service focused on Pentecost. As the organ played, the sound of a brass quartet suddenly filled the air. I remember that trumpets also brought a response from Matthew. He would look up with an alertness or wonderment in his expression, as if to say, "Oh, that's something new."

The sound of the brass in the service brought back another memory: Matthew's joyful laughter. Several years ago, I decided to take up the trumpet (which lasted only a few years). I purchased a horn and took weekly lessons. During one of Matthew's visits home, I began to practice. He looked at me with an expression that said, "I don't believe what I'm hearing!" He listened to another squawk, threw back his head and laughed harder than we had ever heard him laugh. Again and again, he laughed and giggled until we were all in stitches. My novice attempts to play had at least pleased him. Needless to say, these memories brought the tears once again.

Another time, I was driving home and listening to pastor Chuck Swindoll's radio program. During the message, he listed the names of Jesus' disciples. Hearing him say the name *Matthew* brought my sense of loss and sadness to the surface where it stayed for several days. Who would have thought that would have happened?

Then there were times when my feelings were just flat. A low-grade numbness sets in, and I wondered when the pain would hit again. Just three months after Matthew died, I had been very busy with work and projects. For several days, there had been little feeling and no tears. As I told a client what had happened, however, the tears came to my eyes. Then as I sat with the parents of a profoundly disabled child, trying to help them, the tears again rose to the surface. Next, I received a note from a friend who had lost his 19-year-old son in an accident more than four years earlier. When he said the pain was sometimes still as fresh as if it had just happened, I wondered, *Will it be that way for us?* Again my eyes clouded over.

During that dry time, as I refer to it, grief hit hard once more. I was riding my exercise bike and listening to a worship tape by Terry Clark. One of the songs was "I Remember." As I rode, I was also working on a new catalog to send to people who had attended our seminars over the years. I was wondering whether to include anything about Matthew, since most of the people had heard our story. I had considered saying, "For years we had prayed for Matthew to be whole. On March 15, God saw fit to make him whole."

As I thought about that (and perhaps because of the music and the fact that I was planning to visit his grave for the first time), the flood occurred. The sense of loss was overwhelming, and I wept intensely. One thing I've learned: you never need to apologize for your tears.[21]

Years ago, when I wrote some of this chapter and looked once again at some of the notes my wife and I received, and my written thoughts, the feelings and tears rose once more to the surface. I found two written responses to my tears that I had put in a folder. This first one I wrote nine months after Matthew's death:

January 5, 1991

Where have the tears gone? There was a time when I thought they would never end, but now I miss them as though they were a friend. There's only a mist where once a stream, the memories are fading all too fast, like it was last night's dream. It seems too soon to be this way, but I realize they may return yet another day. Who would have thought the sobs and clouded eyes would be missed, but they are. And yet, even as this is written, the words are difficult to see for some strange reason.

The poems and letters from friends help to bring back the loss again. Words of comfort expressed at the time of deepest pain help to keep Matthew's memory alive. For all that we have of him now are memories. Someone else has the joy of his presence, his laugh, his smile and his hugs.

Where have they gone? They haven't. They were hiding and waiting once again for the time to be called out and express the loss. They're here again, not as an intruder, but as a welcomed friend. Please don't stay away so long the next time. I need you. We need you.

Then in the fifteenth month, I wrote:

It's been some time since the feelings came to the surface. You begin to wonder if they ever will again. But then they do. And each time is different. It began with finding some old pictures of Matthew when he was quite young, and in most of them he was smiling. Two days later we were watching Dr. Lloyd Ogilvie on a Sunday morning TV program, and he read the passage in which the centurion came to Jesus about his son who was dying. Jesus told him to go home, his son would live. Both Joyce and I had the same response: "I wish that Jesus would have made that statement to us about Matthew." The tears came that morning. They will always be there and come when you least expect them. But they are there as part of our connection with something that we valued but lost, at least for the present time. They are also a reminder that our life is a series of transitions and changes, some of which we like and others we resist.

You can recover from the loss of your child. It will take an understanding of the grief process and a change of attitude fromthinking, *It will never end, so I will adjust and survive,* and a willingness to make the painful journey through the wilderness of grief.

Most parents want to discover how to cope with their loss. Coping is tied to mourning. Coping means "struggling or contending with some success." An older meaning is "to strike back or fight." Mourning is all about actually and willingly working through your grief, striking or fighting back. It's the process of purging yourself of the grief over your loss.[22] Ann Kasner Stearns wrote, "All of us feel powerless at times because we are human beings. Triumphant survivors, however, trade in the position of helplessness for a decision to take charge and search for options."[23]

A unique factor is involved in the loss of a child. It's perhaps best summarized by the phrase "to never forget." Ronald Knapp describes this as follows:

> One important commonality that appeared to be characteristic of all parents who have suffered the loss of a child for whatever reason took the form of a need that makes the loss of a child different from other kinds of losses, and one that truly complicates the normal process of grieving. This is the need or desire never to forget—or to remember always!
>
> The child is gone! Out of sight! And parents, mothers particularly, harbor a great fear that what memories they have of the child may eventually fade away. They fear that they will forget the sight of the child's face, the sound of his or her voice, the texture of the child's hair, the uniqueness of the hands, even the child's characteristic smell. Parents severely miss these sensual experiences and eventually come to wish to retain them in memory for as long as they live.[24]

As you grieve, keep in mind certain steps that may be helpful. We've already talked about guilt, but a major task is to break the guilt connection. The longer you let it linger, the more it gains a foothold and takes up permanent residence. Self-blame will cripple you and your other family relationships. The guilt may be over something you did, didn't do, thought or wished.

If others around you don't talk about the death or seem to avoid you or the subject, you may feel even guiltier, as though you did something wrong. But people avoid the subject for reasons that have nothing to do with wrong. They avoid the subject for reasons that have nothing to do with blaming you. Most don't know what to say, and many feel anxiety over your child's death. They feel threatened. As a bereaved parent, you represent their worst fears; if it happened to your child, it could happen to theirs.

Unfortunately, such a calloused response leaves you without support and fails to provide the validation you need about what has happened. Nothing hurts more than being ignored.[25]

You may have to take the initiative to break the silence. When you talk about your child and what you experienced, you let others know it's acceptable to discuss the death. If you feel you're being avoided, go to others and start conversations. Use a letter to help people know what you've experienced and how they can respond to you. That makes it easier to bring up the subject.

In a loving, gentle way, you need to let others know that you will not be ignored. Then you will receive more care and support. Many are concerned that talking about your loss will intensify your pain. In some of the caring cards we received, we read statements like, "I hope this letter or card hasn't increased your hurt." But even if it did bring our pain to the surface, the comfort from the card was worth it all. Here are two caring notes that came from one of Matthew's home staff and one of his teachers:

Dear Mr. and Mrs. Wright,

It was a joy working with Matthew. He had such an infectious laugh! He would look at you from the corner of his eye, half-smiling as if to say, "I'm going to make my move when you're not watching me"—which is just what he did! He was becoming more sure of himself, more independent. He had learned to trust me, to let me prompt and encourage him without pulling away as much. This means a great deal to me.

I'll always remember the day Matthew moaned when enjoying a good meal, and the way he loved to splash when taking a bath...

Dear Mr. and Mrs. Wright,

This letter is late coming I know, but it has been very difficult for me to sit down and actually acknowledge the sad fact that Matthew was taken from us. I felt many other ones would be taken before Matthew.

It was just at Christmas time I was remembering taking Matthew and Debra to the mall at Christmas time the year before. He kept trying to sneak off on me, and I would get so tickled at him and the expression he would give me when he saw me behind him. They both, and me too, enjoyed that day so much. Matthew was one that I have missed the most since leaving Dominga School.

I know there is not much I can say, but please realize that Matthew gave so much pleasure to so many and he was a joy for Dominga to have. He was always so neat and clean and full of surprises for us. His absence from school was always a disappointment for us...

What are your sources of support? Find them. Identify them. Don't withdraw even if you feel like doing so, as you will. Find a supporting person(s) and a group such as GriefShare. The person needs to be accessible and available, experienced with a loss similar to yours, able to help you go on with your life, and able to help with tasks and errands you're unable to do during the grieving period.[26] (For support groups, see the appendix at the end of this chapter.)

You can expect something else to occur if and when you struggle with guilt. You're likely to concentrate on how perfect or good your child was. You tend to exalt all your child's positive traits, to idealize him or her. You think of your child as the "best," the "most loving" or the "most special."[27]

As you work through recovery, you may discover that you have developed a new attitude toward death and your own dying. Studies show that parents tend to no longer view death as their enemy. Many find that it could be a friend, especially a parent whose child went through a painful, lingering illness. For them, death became a release and relief. And as they dealt with their child's death, they were able to handle the death of others more effectively. Isn't it interesting that it often takes this experience to make the truth of God's Word become a reality?

As you proceed through your valley of recovery, try these three suggestions that have meant the most to me. First, *pray.* Write out your prayers as you may write out your feelings at times.

Don't edit your prayers; let your feelings flow. Second, *worship*—at home and in church, as though you're the only person there. Don't worry about what others might think of your feelings and tears. Third, *read Scripture.* Let the comfort of God's Word meet your needs. Read comforting passages again and again, to yourself and aloud.

God's words, spoken to us in time of need, give us the ability to survive. Here is a brief collection of promises for those who mourn:

> In all their distress he too was distressed,
> and the angel of his presence saved them.
> In his love and mercy he redeemed them;
> he lifted them up and carried them all the days of old (Isa. 63:9).

> The LORD is my shepherd (Ps. 23:1).

> For God so loved the world that he gave his one and only Son, that whoever believes in him shall not

perish but have eternal life (John 3:16).

I am the resurrection and the life. He who believes in me will live, even though he dies; and whoever lives and believes in me will never die (John 11:25-26).

God will wipe away every tear from their eyes (Rev. 7:17).

He who goes out weeping, carrying seed to sow, will return with songs of joy, carrying sheaves with him (Ps. 126:6).

Come to me, all you who are weary and burdened, and I will give you rest (Matt. 11:28).

Praise be to the God and Father of our Lord Jesus Christ, the Father of compassion and the God of all comfort, who confronts us in all our troubles (2 Cor. 1:3-4).

When you pass through the waters, I will be with you, and when you pass through the rivers, they will not sweep over you. When you walk through the fire, you will not be burned; the flames will not set you ablaze (Isa. 43:2).

The Spirit helps us in our weakness. We do not know what we ought to pray for, but the Spirit himself intercedes for us with groans that words cannot express (Rom. 8:26).

For I am convinced that neither death nor life, neither angels nor demons, neither the present nor the future, nor any powers, neither height nor depth, nor anything else in all creation, will be able to separate us from the love of God that is Christ Jesus our Lord (Rom. 8:38-39).

My grace is sufficient for you, for my power is made perfect in weakness (2 Cor. 12:9).

Ask all the questions you need to ask, again and again.

Often parents, and others, ask, "Where do children go when they die?"

I believe the Scriptures tell us they go to heaven, into the presence of God. David had an infant son who died when he was only seven days old. David's response indicates that he believed his son was somewhere he, too, would go one day. And that somewhere is *heaven.* (John MacArthur's book *Safe in the Arms of God* is a helpful resource.)

When anyone dies, the soul leaves the body. Our bodies are simply "tents." Paul said that when we're away from the body, we're at home with the Lord (see 2 Cor. 5:8). He also seemed to indicate that when Christians die, they awake in glory (see 1 Thess. 4:14).

Be patient with your recovery, but believe that you will recover. David Wiersbe offers this advice about believing:

> In grief God seems to have abandoned us. He hasn't. In grief we feel as if nothing matters. It does. Sometimes we think life is not worth living; it is! In times of sorrow people of faith have to "believe against the grain." In our weakness, God reveals his strength, and we do more than we thought possible.
>
> Faith means clinging to God in spite of circumstances. It means following him when we cannot see, being faithful to him when we don't feel like it.

Mourners need a creed: it is "I believe!" We need to affirm this creed daily:
- I believe God's promises are true.
- I believe heaven is real.
- I believe I will see my child again.
- I believe God will see me through.
- I believe nothing can separate me from God's love.
- I believe God has work for me to do.

"Believing against the grain" means having a survivalist attitude. Bereaved parents are survivors; they have endured. Not only do they survive, but also out of grief they create something good.[28]

In time, as other parents have, you will find meaning in what you've experienced. Listen to the words of these parents:

> I really don't know why this happened to us, but I've stopped looking for the answer! I just have to put my faith in the Lord's hands.... Only He knows—only He has the answers!

> The Lord works in many strange ways. At first I simply could not fathom this, but then I accepted

the Lord.... He must have had His reasons, and these—whatever they are—are good enough for me.

At first I was confused and bewildered and angry. Why did this happen to us? Why did God permit this to happen? ... Then I began to realize that it was the will of God.... Who am I to question further?

Nothing pacified me after Tommy's death. I couldn't understand how a loving God could allow such a thing.... However, I eventually came to realize that God was my greatest salvation; whatever His reasons are for taking Tommy, I can now accept them! I think of Him as holding Tommy in His arms until the day I can join him.

"The Lord giveth and the Lord taketh away"—that is a quote from the Bible! I never knew exactly what it meant until this thing happened.... You're right, I questioned! I was angry and filled with hate over the loss of our son.... However, the anger and hate softened as I accepted the Lord. I put myself in His hands and immediately felt a sense of peace overtake me.[29]

Earlier, I talked about saying goodbye to Matthew. We said it many times, in various ways. Visiting the gravesite is one. Redecorating his room or finally giving away his clothes is another. I've read goodbye letters that some have written to a loved one who has died. But when a young child dies, I believe there's a difference.

When a Christian, or a young child, dies, those who are left behind have to say goodbye. But the one who died is able to say hello to the Lord. This is why our feelings can sometimes be a mixture of sadness for our loss, but joy for what the deceased person is now experiencing. We've felt this. We have a void in our lives, but Matthew's life is now full and complete. The Christian death is a transition, a tunnel leading from this world into the next. This transition can be depicted in many ways.

A month after Matthew died, I received a copy of Max Lucado's inspirational book *The Applause of*

Heaven. I had heard about the book, especially the final chapter. So I did what I normally don't: I went immediately to the final chapter and read it first. In that chapter, the author begin by describing his conclusion to a long trip and finally arriving at the airport. His wife and three daughters are excited that he's home. But one of them has an interesting response. In the midst of the shouts of joy, she stops long enough to clap. She applauds him. Isn't that different? But it's also affirming and appropriate.

Then Max talks about the Christian's ultimate home and homegoing, and what might happen there. He begins by quoting Revelation 21:1-4:

> "Then I saw a new heaven and a new earth, for the first heaven and the first earth had passed away, and there was no longer any sea. I saw the holy City, the new Jerusalem, coming down out of heaven from God, prepared as a bride beautifully dressed for her husband. And I heard a loud voice from the throne saying, 'Now the dwelling of God is with men, and

he will live with them. They will be his people, and God himself will be with them and be their God. He will wipe every tear from their eyes. There will be no more death or mourning or crying or pain, for the old order of things has passed away.'"

John says that someday God will wipe away your tears. The same hands that stretched the heavens will touch your cheeks. The same hands that formed the mountains will caress your face. The same hands that curled in agony as the Roman spike cut through will someday cup your face and brush away your tears forever.

When you think of a world where there will be no reason to cry, ever, doesn't it make you want to go home?

"There will be no more death..." John declares. Can you imagine it? A world with no hearses or morgues or cemeteries or tombstones? Can you imagine a world with no spades of dirt thrown on caskets? No names chiseled into marble? No funerals? No black dresses? No black wreaths?

In the next world, John says, "goodbye" will never be spoken.[30]

Every person on earth is appointed to die at some time. We fear it, resist it, try to postpone it and even deny its existence. But none of that will work. We can't keep our loved ones from dying. We can't keep ourselves from dying. But we can see death from God's perspective. Lucado concludes his book with what homegoing means from a new point of view:

> Before you know it, your appointed arrival time will come; you'll descend the ramp and enter the City. You'll see faces that are waiting for you. You'll hear your name spoken by those you love. And maybe, just maybe—in the back, behind the crowds—the One who would rather die than live without you will remove his pierced hands from his heavenly robe and ... applaud.[31]

I just sat there quietly after reading that, letting it minister to me. I could see Jesus responding that way as

Matthew arrived. It's true—our loved ones who have died are saying hello. We have said goodbye to them. It's true—we say hello to each day without them, but only for now!

Grief Support Groups

GriefShare—Grief Recovery Support Group—located at churches throughout the country. Go to www.griefshare.org and click on "Find a Group" to find a GriefShare near you.

The Compassionate Friends
P.O. Box 3696
Oakbrook, IL 60522
630-990-0010

DC Candlelighters, Childhood Cancer Foundation
P.O. Box 2324
Centreville, VA 20122

The National Sudden Infant Death Syndrome Foundation
(SIDS)
800-221-SIDS

National SUID/SIDS Resource Center

www.sidscenter.orb/about.html

Recommended Resources

Nadine Galinsky, *When a Grandchild Dies: What to Do, What to Say, How to Cope* (Houston, TX: Gal in Sky Publishing, 1999)

John MacArthur, *Safe in the Arms of God: Truth from Heaven About the Death of a Child* (Nashville, TN: Thomas Nelson, 2003)

Mary Lou Reed, *Grandparents Cry Twice: Help for Bereaved Grandparents* (Amityville, NY: Baywood Publishing, 2000)

4

Helping Children in Grief

While everyone in a family grieves, we leave out some and neglect their pain. Children are the forgotten grievers in our country. Adults seem to receive all the attention, while children are left out of the equation. Children not only grieve, but their grief is different from that of an adult. But whatever loss you have experienced, your children have experienced it in some way as well.

A child's grief comes out in the middle of everyday life. It can't be predicted.

A child can put grief aside more quickly. One question may be about her grandfather's death, and the next response is about her doll.

A child's grief comes out in brief but intense episodes.

Children express their grief in actions. They are limited in their verbal expression, depending upon their age.

They often postpone their grief or part of it.

Childhood grief often lasts throughout childhood, and pieces of it last into adulthood, since they don't have an adult's ability to grieve.

Children grieve differently from adults. Instead of experiencing ongoing intense distress, many children are likely at first to deny death and then grieve intermittently for many years.

This is why it's so critical to communicate with a child when there's a loss. They need information, and getting information solves many issues for them.

Information tames their fears. By talking with your children about death and grief, you can re-create a secure place so that they can learn to trust the world again.

Information gives children a sense of control. When they feel confused and besieged by new emotions, they need to be anchored by you, the adult.

Information gives your child permission to express feelings they want to communicate. They don't grieve on command, and they need the freedom to come to you at any time.

Information helps children prepare for future losses. Most adults have never been prepared for this. Sheltered children can't cope as well as those who understand the truth of life.

If you don't talk to them, they'll talk to themselves and fill in the blanks! Imagination and other children are not good resources during a time of grief.[1]

How to Help a Child Grieve

It is important for an adult to identify what may inhibit a child's ability to grieve the losses he or she experiences. There are several factors that contribute to this problem:
- Parents have difficulty grieving past or current losses.
- Parents are unable to handle and accept their child's expressions of painful experiences. They just don't know how to respond.
- Children are worried about how their parents are handling the loss and attempt to protect them.

- Children become overly concerned with maintaining control and feeling secure, and they may feel frightened or threatened by the grief.
- Parents do not caringly prod, stimulate and encourage their children to grieve.
- Children don't have the security of a loving, caring environment.
- In the case of a loved one's death, children may question their role in making it happen. Their misplaced guilt is further enhanced if they have ambivalent feelings toward the loved one.
- Families fail to acknowledge and discuss the reality of death or loss.[2]

Which of these factors are characteristic of your family? Regardless of the type of loss children experience, the following seven steps are important in the grieving process:

1. Children need to accept the loss, experience the pain and express their sorrow.
2. Children require assistance to identify and express the wide range of feelings they're experiencing.

3. Children need to know why others are sad and why they themselves are sad. Acknowledging these feelings lets a child know that it's *okay* to be sad. Tell them, "This is how we feel when someone dies."
4. Children must be told that it is the death that has made people sad. Without an explanation, they may think others' sadness is caused by something they did or didn't do. Start by saying, "This is a very, very sad time"; "A very, very sad thing has happened"; "Mommy and Daddy are sad because..."; "People at church are sad because..."
5. Children need encouragement to remember and review their relationship with the loved one.
6. Children need help in learning to relinquish and say goodbye to what they lost.
7. Children respond differently to loss depending on their age and level of emotional maturity.

A Child Is Never Too Young to Feel Grief

Grief is not just for adults or adolescents. Children of all ages experience grief. Let's consider these various age groups.

Infants

Grieving occurs even in very young infants. Young children between four months and two years of age express distress when responding to a loss. At this stage, separation from the mother is a significant loss. If the separation is sudden, the child will express shock and protest. Prolonged separation creates despair and sadness. The child loses interest in objects and activities that are usually pleasurable. Unless a caring individual steps into the vacated role, the infant will become detached from everyone.

Keep in mind, too, that no matter how young children are when someone close dies, they are still impacted by the loss throughout their life. They may have no memories of the deceased, but they have experienced the loss of someone with whom they shared a significant bond. As members of a family, they are also impacted by the grief of other family members.

Toddlers to Preschoolers

Children between the ages of two to five may show their grief in a number of ways. Because they don't understand the significance of the loss, they may ask seemingly useless questions, again and again. They may ask, "Hasn't he been dead long enough?" Concepts take time to understand, and the concept of death hasn't been fully formed yet in the child's mind.

A child in this age range may appear bewildered and tend to regress in behavior, becoming demanding and clinging. If what was lost is not returned, expressions of anger increase. You may need to assist the child toward acknowledging and expressing feelings of loss. Many adults, unfortunately, make the mistake of removing a child from familiar surroundings following a family death or trauma. This further undermines the child's sense of security and raises his or her anxiety.

In the case of death, children at this age are obsessed with thoughts of the lost loved one and overwhelmed by an intense sadness. They tend to idealize this person, dwelling on reviewing and remembering their lost relationship.

Ages Three to Six

Children between the ages of three to six engage in what is known as magical thinking. They believe their thoughts can influence people and events. For example, a child who is upset about a parent taking a trip may wish that the car would get a flat tire so that the parent doesn't leave. Then when the parent is killed in a car crash caused by a blowout, the child feels responsible.

Additionally, this is an age when fears increase. Children become aware of threatening events in the world around them. They're curious about bodily functions. When they experience the death of a loved one, children may ask questions like: "Can he still eat?" "Can she go potty?" "Does he cry?" "Will she get out of the box and hug me again?" and "Will he be a ghost?"

At this age, children don't understand the permanency of death. For them, it's reversible. E.T. came back from the dead. So did Jesus and Lazarus. And so does Wile E. Coyote in the *Road Runner* cartoons. They may think that if you wish hard enough, a person will come back to life.

When a pet dies, young children may act as if it is still alive by calling it, asking to feed it or looking under a bed for it. These kids see people and animals as cartoon characters—able to survive anything. To them, death is merely a deep and temporary sleep. Parents often reinforce this misconception by telling them that the dead person is "resting" or "just didn't wake up." Even some of the terminology used by funeral homes reinforces the denial of the permanency of death, for example, the "slumber room."[3]

Children in this age group often focus their attention on one detail of an experience and ignore everything

else. They have difficulty seeing the whole picture clearly. They don't comprehend the significance of loss. For example, if Grandpa dies, they may ask or think:
- *Does this mean someone else is going to die?*
- *Grandpa died from a headache. Mommy says that she has a headache too...*
- *Old people die. Daddy is very old, so Daddy may die too...*

Also be prepared for indirect questions aimed at finding out if someone else *might* die, such as, "How old are you?" or "How old is Daddy?" You must also be able to explain the difference between:
- very, very sick; and just sick
- very, very old; and "old" as in more than 20
- very old and very sick; and very old and not sick[4]

Ages Five to Eight

As children grow older, usually between the ages of five and eight, they develop the ability to understand loss, and even death. They're especially vulnerable because they can grasp the significance of their losses but have limited skills to cope with those losses.

They often look on death as a "taker"—something that comes and gets you. The question "Who killed him?" is common. They may accept death as a reality but not the fact that everyone is going to die. One of the worst prayers that has been taught to children over the years (including to me) was:

> *Now I lay me down to sleep, I pray the Lord my soul to keep; if I should die before I wake, I pray the Lord my soul to take. Amen.*

What damage does this do to young children?

When faced with loss, children may use denial as a coping mechanism. It's easier to act as if nothing has happened. Children also hide their feelings at this age because they don't want to look like a baby. Afraid of becoming out of control, children may vent their feelings only when alone. To others, they may appear insensitive, uncaring and unaffected by the loss, which leaves the parent unaware of the extent of their grief.

At this age, children need to be encouraged, again and again, to vent their feelings. Allowing children to see their parents grieve and talking about their own feelings can help children work though their grief.

A Child's Varying Reactions to Loss

The death of a loved one is an extremely difficult loss for all of us to handle. But for children, it is even more difficult because they lack the resources to handle such a serious loss. Let's consider a child's reaction to a serious loss such as death.

Fear

Children who experience the death of a loved one can experience a number of fears, including the following:
- *Fear of losing the other parent, siblings or grandparents*—they tend to see the remaining family members as candidates for death.

- *Fear of their own death*—this is especially true if the child is younger than the sibling who died or is approaching the age at which the sibling died.
- *Fear of going to sleep because they equate sleep with death*—even the prayer "If I should die before I wake..." reinforces this misconception. Dreams and nightmares intensify the fear.
- *Fear of separation because of the perceived insecurity of the home and family*—they no longer feel safe and protected. They're hesitant to talk about their feelings because it may upset the other family members. One young girl told me, "When Daddy died, I wanted to talk to my mother about it. But I was afraid to because it made her cry, and I didn't want the others yelling at me 'cause I did that."

Guilt

The second feeling associated with grief is guilt. It is difficult to identify all of the sources of guilt, but there seem to be three main reasons why children experience guilt when loved ones die:

1. "They died because I did something wrong. I misbehaved!" Children have a knack for remembering things they've done that they think are wrong. They may have made a mistake, broken something or forgotten to say or do something. Just like adults, children can end up with an incredible list of "if only" thoughts or regrets.
2. "I wanted them dead. I thought it, and it happened." It is important to remember that young children believe they can actually make things happen by thinking them. It's easy for kids to think their anger or aggression killed the loved one. Because they take on this responsibility, they live in fear of being found out and punished.
3. "I didn't love them enough." It is common for children to believe that if you love someone enough, it will keep them from dying. They long for a second chance to make things right.

Anger

Another common grief response is anger. A number of beliefs trigger children's anger. They often feel abandoned and left to face life on their own. They're angry because their future has been dramatically changed—they won't be with that special person anymore. They feel victimized by events that are out of their control.

Children may be angry at their parents for these reasons:
- For not telling them that the person who died was so sick;
- For spending so much time with the sick person—they feel neglected and isolated; and
- For just needing someone to be angry with.[5]

Kids express their anger in different ways. It may be targeted like a well-aimed bullet or sprayed in all directions like a shotgun pellet. It may be directed at family members, friends, teachers, pets or even at God. It may be expressed in tantrums, fights, silent hostility or verbal blasts. As difficult as it may be to experience these demonstrative expressions of anger, it is a healthy sign. The alternative response—bottling up the anger—can result in digestive problems and depression.

Confusion

Worth mentioning here is the sense of confusion that can accompany the loss of a loved one. Just imagine that you are a six-year-old child who has been raised in a Christian home, and your mother dies. You probably wonder, *Where is God? Why didn't He keep my mother alive? Why didn't He make her well? My uncle told me Mom went to be with God. Why'd He do that?* Not only are children confused about God, but they are also dealing with a mixture of feelings about the person who died.

They are trying to sort through mixed messages and advice they receive from grown-ups. The expectations of adults often create confusion. One adult may be implying, *Oh, you poor little child. You must feel so sad and alone.* At the same time, someone else may be giving the message, *Now you're the man in the family. You'll have to be strong.* The child will feel confused by these conflicting messages that say to be strong, sad, in control, a help to others, and so on.

The child's memories of the deceased can cause confusion. The survivors are talking about the person in a way that conflicts with the child's memories. They are praising and lauding the person's perfect qualities in a way the child cannot understand. The child may wonder, *Was Mom really as perfect as they say? I didn't know that. Sometimes I didn't even like her, and I thought she was bad when she yelled and went on and on. Maybe I was wrong. I hope no one finds out what I think.* You can see how this would create confusion as well as guilt for the child.

The fluctuating moods of others also generate confusion. Individuals around the child may be cheerful one moment and moody and quiet the next. While this is a normal response, the child is seeking stability and assurance from these people, but their changing moods cause the child to question his or her own responses. The child may ask himself or herself, *Is it me? Did I do something wrong? Do they want me around or not?*[6]

When a death occurs, you can expect some of the following:
- The emotional responses and behaviors of children vary around the time of loss. They are strongly influenced by the reactions of the surviving parent as well as other adults.
- When a parent is in a terminal condition, the least likely to know are the younger children.
- Recapturing memories of the funeral and being able to talk about it increase over time for most children.
- Children who are prepared for the funeral are better able to handle it than those children who weren't given any prior information.
- Including children in the planning of the funeral has a positive effect. It helps them to feel important and useful at a time when many are feeling overwhelmed.
- Children who are involved want the funeral to reflect the life of the

parent more than focus on the loss itself or the afterlife.
- Children should be given a choice about attending the wake, funeral or burial. These need to be informed choices by children who are prepared for what they will see and experience.
- Visiting the grave helps children remain connected with the dead parent. There's a huge vacancy in their life. This is a time when they are working through what place the deceased parent has in their current life.[7]

Preparing Children for Loss

To cope well with loss, children should be told what is going to happen and what they are going to experience. Should they be brought to the funeral home, the service or both? Definitely—if they are well prepared in advance. Tell them what will happen, and then give them the choice of going or not. Fit the following explanation around your family's plans and special traditions:

_____ will be taken from _____, where he died, to the funeral home. At the funeral home, _____ will be dressed in clothes that he (she) liked and put into a casket. A casket is a box we use so that when _____ is buried, no dirt will get on him (her). Because _____'s body isn't working anymore, it won't move or do any of the things it used to do. But it will look like _____ always did.

People will come and visit us and say how sorry they are that _____ died. After _____ days the casket will be closed and taken to the church, where people will say prayers for the family. Then we will go to the cemetery where _____ will be buried in a place that _____ picked out.

If you like, you can come to the funeral home and visit for a while—and even go to the cemetery. You could bring something to leave with _____ if you want; that would be nice.

We have to go to the funeral home to make plans, and we'll let you know all about them when we come back. We will be gone for _____ hours.

For a cremation, use this additional information:

After we leave the funeral home, _____ will be taken to a crematory, a place where his (her) body will be turned into ashes. Then we will take those ashes and _____ (scatter them; keep them in an urn). Since _____'s body doesn't work and doesn't feel anything, being cremated doesn't hurt.

In addition, if the dead person has changed because of illness or accident, it is important to describe some of this change (e.g., "It's still Grandpa, but you know he was sick and lost a lot of weight—so he will look thinner").[8]

Keep Children Connected

Children who remain connected after the loss are better able to talk about the dead parent. They can talk to family members as well as others. They are likely to try to please the dead parent with their behavior.

It is important to have a relationship with the dead parent. This is part of the continuing process called constructing. The constructing process involves discovering the meaning of this loss rather than just letting go of their parent; this discovering continues to be a part of the child's life experience.[9]

Describe the Event

Here are six examples of how to describe to young children how and why a death has occurred:
1. *Old Age:* "When a person gets very, very, very old, his body wears out and stops working."
2. *Terminal Illness:* "Because the disease couldn't be stopped, the person got very, very sick, his body wore out and stopped working."
3. *Accident:* "A terrible thing happened (car crash, and so on). His body was badly hurt and couldn't be fixed. It stopped working."
4. *Miscarriage:* "Sometimes when a baby is just starting to grow, something happens that makes it

stop. We don't know what it was; it wasn't anything anyone did."
5. *Stillborn:* "Sometimes something makes the baby die before it is born. We're not sure why, but it's nothing anybody did or didn't do."
6. *Sudden Infant Death Syndrome (SIDS):* "Sometimes with little babies something makes their bodies stop working. It's nothing anybody did or forgot to do. Doctors are not sure why it happens."[10]

How can we help our children learn to handle the losses of life? Start early. Overprotection and denial rob children of the opportunity to develop the skills they'll need throughout their lives.

Here are 11 guidelines for helping a child handle the loss when a death occurs.

1. Give Your Children Permission to Grieve and

Encourage Them to Talk and Ask Questions

Whether the loss is the death of a family member, a major move or the loss of a pet, your children need permission to mourn. For certain children, permission may not be enough. Some need an invitation to share their feelings, but they also need to be taught how to express sorrow. A few sensitive, well-directed questions can draw them out. If your child still doesn't talk, don't force it. Just let him or her know you're available and ready to listen when they want to talk. You may wish to look for other ways for them to express what they're feeling.

Once children begin to talk about their feelings, it may seem like you've untapped a gusher. They are—in their limited capacity—attempting to make sense of what has happened and regain their security. Children whose questions are answered and who are given a forum for discussion have less need to fantasize and are much easier to help than non-expressive children. If your children don't share their feelings, watch for indirect questions or statements of concern and try to put their feelings into words for them.[11]

2. Be Available When Your Child Is Ready to Grieve

Being available may be the most important element in helping children grieve. Children need affection and a sense of security. Touching them and making eye contact will provide comfort and reassurance. Let the children know that it is normal to have ups and downs. They are not going crazy. Help them break the mourning into manageable pieces so that they don't get overwhelmed. Using illustrations and word pictures can help them identify and talk about their feelings.

Some helpers are surprised to find that children will have the same range of emotions as they do. These emotions include anger, panic, numbness, sadness and guilt. But the children are only starting to identify their emotions and learning what to do about them. Children need others to help them identify their feelings and the sources of those feelings, and express them in constructive ways.

The author of *The Grieving Child* suggests the following ways that helpers and parents can help children express themselves emotionally:

> For the most part, children deal with feelings through some kind of acting out, sometimes in a disruptive manner, yet there are simple ways that you can help your child identify and express feelings.
>
> Look around your child's room, note the materials she is comfortable with, and then see if these can be used as tools in teaching her about feelings. These materials might include paper, crayons, markers, clay, paper bags, puppets, dolls, old magazines, scrapbooks, balloons, a diary, a tape recorder, books or music. The key is that she be familiar with them and comfortable in using them. With some suggestions from you she can turn these materials into drawings, writings, collages, sculptures, plays, scrapbooks or

tapes: all centered on her feelings about the death of a loved one, helping her to express those feelings and to cope appropriately with them. In the course of these exercises she will learn lessons that she will carry into adulthood and possibly pass on to her own children.[12]

You may want to obtain the book *Fears, Doubts, Blues and Pouts* (for children 4 and up) to help your child learn about his or her feelings in a positive way. (You can order it from Christian Marriage Enrichment, www.hnormanwright.com or call 800-875-7560.)

3. Respond with Age-Appropriate Answers

Remember the child's age. Children can't grasp what we can, and if we respond with an adult answer to a child's question, the answer is over their head and ability to understand. If a child is in a state of shock or crisis, his or her thinking ability is lessened even more. It's important that children receive simple, concrete answers to their questions.

4. Give Them Opportunities for Creative Expression

Children who have difficulty verbalizing their feelings may find it easier to express them on paper. Drawing is an effective way for them to gain control over their emotional pain and eventually eliminate it. When the loss is a death, drawing is especially important because it allows children to actually see what their feelings look like. This action helps give them a sense of understanding and control.

Writing or journaling also is beneficial for children whose writing skills are developed. It is easier for them to express on paper the reality of what's happened and their fantasies about it. Writing a letter to the deceased person or even to God can be helpful. Encourage your children to read aloud and discuss what they've written, but remember to respect their privacy. The choice whether or not to share needs to be theirs.

5. Create Opportunities for Playtime

Periodically, the child needs to be encouraged to take a break from his or her grief and to play with friends. Play is an important type of expression for children, especially for younger children whose verbal skills are limited. In the safety of play, a child can vent various feelings. Play helps them regain a feeling of safety and security. It gives them a feeling of power over the effects of loss and allows them to separate themselves from what has happened.[13] Watch what they do and say during their play.

They may feel like they're betraying the deceased if they have fun or allow themselves some enjoyment. But play is a normal and beneficial part of their lives and gives them time to recuperate. It also helps them realize that life goes on. Encourage playtime with peers and adults.

6. Watch Your Expectations

Everyone needs to be careful not to overprotect a child. Lecturing or making decisions for them is not helpful while they're coping with a loss. When possible, it is better if they learn to make their own choices and are allowed to grow through the experiences of their lives.

The flip side of this issue, though, is that parents often have expectations that are inappropriate for their children's age level. I've overheard parents or other adults say to a child, "You're going to have to take over now and be the man of the family (or be the strong one)." This is an unrealistic expectation and places too much of a burden on the child. These kinds of messages will short-circuit the child's grieving process. Children need to be given age-appropriate responsibilities.

7. Dismiss Their Myths

It is important to discover if the child has been practicing magical thinking. Younger children are particularly vulnerable to this.

Children will often be impatient with themselves because they feel sad longer than they think they should. They also feel that no one has ever felt the way they do, so they may feel uncomfortable with their friends. They need to be told not to expect too much of themselves or others at this time; they need encouragement to talk with their friends—especially those who have experienced similar losses. Communicating with children of all ages normalizes what they're experiencing.

8. Make Honesty a Policy

While grieving, children look to adults for hope and encouragement. When children ask adults questions, adults need to avoid giving them platitudes and let them know it is all right to ask why when bad things happen. Adults need to admit that they don't have all the answers, but they will get through it together. One mother told her six-year-old son, "I know it is a sad time for you. We are all sad and wish things were different. There are many changes happening right now, but in time things will settle down. Someday the pain will go away. It may go away gradually and keep returning again and again, but as we help and love one another, it is going to go away."[14]

When there's been a death, discuss whether or not this is the child's first experience with death. If it is, the child will need help to understand the loss and sort out his or her feelings about it. Be especially sensitive to your child's reactions and anticipate the unexpected. Use words and phrases your child can easily understand. It may help to rehearse what you plan to say with someone else first.

How would you answer a five-year-old child who asks, "What does 'dead' mean?" How would you answer that question at her level? Always be clear and as factual as possible, telling the truth about the death and what caused it. When children ask questions, give them accurate information such as, "Your brother's heart stopped beating and that is why he died." It is better to use proper death language such as,

"Grandpa died," rather than, "Grandpa passed away." However, be sensitive about how many details you give. If you have no answer to their question, then say so. Let them know that when you do have an answer, you will share it with them.

The authors of *How Do We Tell the Children?* offer an example of this type of questioning and how to respond:
- "Will Grandpa ever move again?" (No, his body has stopped working.)
- "Why can't they fix him?" (Once the body stops working, it can't start again.)
- "Why is he cold?" (The body only stays warm when it's working.)
- "Why isn't he moving?" (He can't move because his body isn't working anymore.)
- "When will he come back?" (He won't. People who die don't come back.)
- "Is he sleeping?" (No. When we sleep, our body is still working, just resting.)
- "Can he hear me?" (No. He could only hear you if his body was working.)

- "Can he eat after he is buried?" (No, a person eats only when his body is working.)[15]

9. Allow Children to Respond in Their Own Way

Don't expect children to respond as adults. Initially, they may not seem upset or sad. Young children even may have difficulty remembering the deceased. They may need help to remember their relationship with the deceased before they can resolve their grief. Photos and videos are helpful. Reminiscing about times spent together and reviewing certain qualities of the person also may be helpful. Part of your ministry will be helping parents know how to respond.

Children often regress because they don't know how to grieve. The important thing is to allow children to progress at their own rate. Adults need to be available to observe their reactions. If they begin to express strong feelings, encourage them; don't block them. Allow them to cry or express anger or even bitterness. In time, they will probably begin to ask questions. Answer them simply and honestly, even though you may struggle with them yourself, whether you're a parent, pastor or counselor.

10. Watch for Signs of Fear

Children need reassurance that their family still exists and that they are important parts of it. Children will tend to ask the same questions over and over again. Their questioning may become intense as they attempt to assimilate what has happened and how it will affect their lives. Parents and counselors may need an abundance of patience to answer them again and again in a loving way.[16]

Children will most likely become aware of their vulnerability to losing other important people or things as they evaluate how this loss will affect their life. Anything of importance to them could become the object of fear. It may be their home, school, friends, church, pets, a daily routine, an activity or another loved one. They will require constant and consistent reassurance. It is important to discuss with children in advance if there are any planned changes in the future.

11. Encourage Children to Continue Normal Routines

It helps if children continue certain family routines. Routines provide security and let them know there are certain constants in their lives—things they can rely on to stay the same.

One of the most practical things to do is to encourage children to take good care of themselves—to get plenty of rest and exercise, and to eat balanced meals.

Final Thought

Loss is a natural and inevitable part of life. A key element in your child's emotional development is learning to deal with the feelings associated with loss and growing through the experience. Parents who guide their children through the troubled waters of the grief process will better equip them to handle the losses of their adult life.

5

The Death of a Parent

The death of a parent is the most common form of bereavement for an adult. In a sense, it is expected, but we still resist its occurrence.

The older we become, the better we understand that our parents will die. We accept that they won't be around forever. Perhaps as we age and our bodies don't work as well, this reality sets in a bit more. But it's still hard to imagine life without parents. We can foresee their death but don't want to accept its inevitability. As Alexander Levy notes in *The Orphaned Adult:*

> There is no experience quite as stunning as when there is nothing where something has always been. To try and imagine the absence of something is to imagine the thing itself, not the hole left behind. Especially when that thing has the first face you probably ever saw,

spoke the first words you ever heard, and whose touch has comforted and guided and corrected and made you safe since the beginning of time. Parents just are. They are a constant in the lives of their children.[1]

The significance of this loss for you is dependent on many factors. If your relationship with your parent was positive, your grief will be different than a child's whose relationship was negative, unsatisfactory or even ambivalent. How would you describe your relationship with your parents? How would you describe your siblings' relationship?

There are a number of factors that will impact your grief, among them your age and the age of your parents when they died. If your parents were young, you may feel robbed and cheated. If your parents were older, you probably experienced a role reversal with caretaking. Their life circumstances will also impact you. If your mother or father was enjoying life and being productive, no matter their age, you question the death. *Why now? Why them?* But if their health was seriously deteriorating, you will probably feel a sense of relief.

Another factor that will affect you is if this is the first parent you've lost or the second. Many adult children struggle because they've not experienced death or grief before. I remember arriving home from work, at the age of 22, and my wife said my uncle had called and I was to call him at my parents' number. I remember his voice saying, "Your dad was killed in an auto accident driving home from work." I was in shock and stayed that way for days. I didn't know how to respond or act, or what to do. It felt like part of my life had been cut out, like it was over. And I didn't know what to do for my mother, especially since this was the second husband she had lost to a violent death.

How you cope with the death of your parent can depend upon several factors. Your parent could have died after a lingering illness, which may have prepared you for his or her death, and you accepted it in advance. But this could have also created stress in the entire family. You may have been exhausted if you were a caregiver. If it was sudden and violent, you may be in the throes of a crisis or trauma.

You may feel isolated if you are an only child or estranged from siblings. This can happen even if you're married, since your spouse does not have the same loss experience as you. Often a spouse is not as supportive as a good friend. Your spouse may be afraid he or she is losing the spouse he or she knew. Your spouse may be frustrated with you because of his or her deep commitment to you and desire to help and protect you.

What if your parents were divorced? This complicates the grieving process and often the details of the service, as well as your parent's effects and inheritance.

If you are or have experienced other major stresses at this time, or before the death, your grieving could be interrupted, intensified or prolonged. When a parent dies during other changes, it's difficult to believe that you're going to be able to survive everything.[2]

When you lose one parent, it's like you're waiting for the other one to die. Your childhood is almost over. As one person said, "My surviving parent was my last opportunity available to mend our relationship or come to terms with it."

If this was the first parent to die, you are faced with how to respond to your remaining parent or stepparent, or both. In addition to your grief, you may have inherited a number of new responsibilities for your remaining parent or some struggles with your siblings. You may struggle with your feelings about the one who died and the one who was left behind.

Your original family as you knew it is now gone. It has changed. It requires a reorganization of your relationship with whoever is left. Some have said, "I never really thought of my mother as just an individual. I always saw her as part of a couple. It was them. Now it's her and her alone. Who is she by herself? I'm struggling with how to adjust to her by herself."

It's not uncommon for childhood sibling conflicts to emerge once again at this time. Resentment and anger could come to the surface, especially if one sibling felt he or she did more than the others to care for the parent, or if one begins to assume the role of the deceased parent. If your remaining parent needs care, who will be responsible for his or her care?

Additional Losses After Losing a Parent

All major losses carry with them a number of secondary losses as well. Your parents had a unique role in your life. Who you are today comes from them. Your mom and dad are part of you in one way or another. You have some of their good and bad habits. They helped you form who you are, whether you realize it or not. Your feelings, thoughts, hopes, desires, attitudes, values and morals were shaped to some degree by your parents.

Was your parent a protector in some way? If so, who fills that role now?

If your parent was a provider, who fills that role now?

If your parent was a problem solver, who fills that role now?

If your parent was an advisor, who fills that role now?

If your parent was a nurturer, who fills that role now?

If your parent was a comforter, who fills that role now?

Perhaps these were roles that your parent(s) fulfilled in part, but now their memories have resurfaced. One of your other losses is the loss of some of your ties to your past and your childhood. Your parents may be the only ones who know your history. They were your historians, and when they died you lost all of that. As one man said, "I felt like someone stripped me of the history of my life, especially my early years." We end up with unremembered parts of life.

Then there's the buffer between you and death. No matter your age, you've now become the older generation. And if this death was the last parent, you may feel like you're an orphan. It means you can no longer go home, whether it's physically or psychologically. Sometimes the loss of the original home becomes a major loss as well.

Perhaps you regret that you can't make up for deficits in your past relationship; or maybe you feel grief for not being able to make life better for them. Do any of these losses sound familiar? If so, each loss needs to be faced and grieved over. Keep in mind that when you grieve the deaths of your parents, you not only grieve for them but for yourself—for what you have lost with their deaths.

Don't expect others to fully understand what this loss means to you. Unless others knew you well and the level of your involvement with your parents, they don't know exactly what you lost when your parents died. You may have a number of friends who never met your parents. The loss of others' understanding, as well as support, is yet another loss you may have to contend with. Sometimes it's your family members who aren't that supportive since they don't feel the loss as you do. It may be your spouse or children or even siblings. You can't expect others to mourn as you do for someone they didn't know like you did.

Others may be more concerned about you.[3]

There is another loss that many of us feel, which a leading grief therapist describes so well:

> So with the death of your parent you may feel the loss of the perfect and unconditional love that only a parent is supposed to be capable of supplying. You lose someone to validate you and your accomplishments in the way that only a parent, to whom you have wanted to prove yourself, can. If you do not feel you have already done so, you also lose the opportunities to prove yourself once and for all. Our parents, besides being our caretakers, usually have been our primary providers of praise and the permission givers in our lives. Even when we mature enough not to require this from them, seldom does recognition from others mean more.[4]

Rebuilding the Family Structure

The death of a family member not only shakes your life to the core, but it also shakes your family structure. Sometimes the vacancy created by the death of a loved one continues and isn't filled, or it's filled quickly, and others pretend there's no longer a hole in the structure.

A death can be very revealing about the structure of your family strengths, flaws, weaknesses, family secrets, fears, struggles, and so on, or some or all come to the surface for all to see. It's also an opportunity to rebuild. Changes can reshape the family in a positive way and, perhaps, help them find a closeness they never before experienced.

As one author said, "We all live by family folklore." Everyone plays some type of role. You may be aware of your role, or perhaps not.

Your own family structure took years to get to the place it's at now, and many parts of it are deeply entrenched.

The structure is difficult to change, but a death can have a shattering effect.

The death of a parent is one of the great shocks to the family system. The balance that was there is broken. And the roles that each played have been "contorted and enlarged by the power of death."[5]

We all have expectations for ourselves and others about how we "should" respond to the death of a parent. You may feel misunderstood by other family members. They may feel misunderstood by you as well.

Different members of the family, as well as friends, have different ways of expressing their grief. Consider this statement:

> When a parent dies, the adult children can be forced to confront the truth about family relationships. Any ambivalence you may have felt toward one another is brought to the fore, and a lifetime of hidden resentments and regrets are ripped open to create fresh wounds. There is often the fallout of a lifetime of words spoken and left unspoken.

In other cases, there may be a continuation of normal patterns, except they may grow more intractable. One of the children—the one who was the most sensitive to the parent—may carry the banner for the others, becoming the stand-in for the parent's values.

The child who tries to build a shrine to the parent might be offended when others in the family want to tear that shrine down. The sibling who insists that the best way to cope is to accept the loss and just move on might be confronted angrily by the one who wants to hold fast to grief.[6]

Dealing with Major Decisions

Unfortunately, at a time when you're in some of your greatest pain, you may have to make some major decisions, and often not everyone is in agreement with some of the decisions. What about the disposal of property or possessions, or what will happen to the remaining parent, especially if he or she is elderly?

Hopefully your parent(s) left a trust or will with complete instructions. If not, hopefully those now in charge will be able to cooperate and not interfere with everyone's grieving process.

If there is a remaining parent, you still have lost both, in one sense. Your parent has lost a spouse and will not be the same as he or she was before the loss. The remaining parent may not grieve the way you expect or want. Your relationship with him or her has changed. He may seem distant. If his loved one died following years of caregiving, he will experience relief along with his loss. So will you.

In the midst of the pain and grief, consider this as an opportunity for the family to rebuild in a new way, a more positive way. Consider how the relationships can be reformed and reshaped.[7]

Dealing with Family Secrets

What about family secrets? Everyone seems to have them—sometimes it may seem appropriate to keep them, but this could be a false foundation for the family functioning. What do you know about the parent who died, and what don't you know? Some secrets may be negative, and some may be positive. Secrets tend to be something a family member hides because of the consequences of its becoming known.

You may have secrets you never shared with your parents. Sometimes a parent or a child had planned to share some day but never got around to it. Remember, the more secrets a family has, the more closed the family becomes and often the more regrets they experience. Some children are carrying the burden of knowing the secret, but others don't know, or they wonder if others do know. No one talks about it.

Some secrets are life changing, while others may be humorous. Many have failed to realize how kept secrets have made a difference in the relationships.[8]

I Feel Like a Middle-Aged Orphan

Someone said that losing a parent is the new midlife crisis. Just when many are getting their lives fully established and settled, it happens. It's never the right time when your parent dies. For many, a parent's death comes during their middle years.

Most of us struggle with the death of our parent, no matter our age or circumstances. Your parent is irreplaceable. This is a person or persons you've known longer than anyone else in your life. They are the first ones you depended on. You're here today because of them, whether they were good for you or not. Most other relationships in life can be replaced. Who you are today is because of who your parents were. But right now you're probably experiencing an empty feeling. Perhaps you were a fortunate one and experienced unconditional love and acceptance. This is now gone except for your memory of it. It could be that what your mother and father gave was minimal. You may be an adult child with an empty spot and are always searching for a way to be satisfied. But now that opportunity is gone.

Whenever our parent dies, we may begin to really feel our mortality for the first time. As one man said, "As long as my dad was alive, I could believe there was no end." A woman said, "As strange as it sounds, I forgot my mother's age and didn't bother to ask. I didn't want to know, because I didn't want to ever think of her dying."

When a parent dies, opportunities are gone. You may be feeling that now. The trip you wanted to take together, the talk you never got around to having, the questions you always wanted to ask but were hesitant to, the opportunity to ask their forgiveness or the hope they would ask yours. Perhaps you have regrets at this time.

Recognizing that at the loss of both parents we really have become an orphan is a shock to many. And orphans, according to the dictionary, are bereaved of parents. For those who are middle age and above, it's difficult to think of oneself as an orphan.

A Sense of Emptiness and Abandonment

When the last parent dies, there's an aloneness like you've never experienced before. There's a void in your life like never before. For many of us, our earliest and most important memories started with mother and father. All of our other relationships are built on these. We're imprinted with our parents and we follow them and their guidance.

For many it feels like they begin an entirely new life when their parents die. Your parent's absence can be felt in so many venues.[9]

Many begin to both experience and make changes in their life.

When parents die, a person mourns his or her family of origin. I've heard many describe the experience as a sense of emptiness and abandonment. Some feel they have lost their past. They've lost touch with their family history. When parents die, you have multiplied grief: It's not just limited to the death of the person; it's your own youth and mortality as well. Who's there to tell the stories about the past? Rituals are a major part of the grief process, and it's all right to have them. The more rituals you have and use at a time of death, the better the recovery seems to be during the grief process. As Jane Brooks states in *Midlife Orphan:*

> How we deal with the last parent's death is often quite different from the way that we handled the first parent's death. Minus a surviving parent, it is up to the adult orphan, either alone or with family members, to make decisions about the way the last parent will be memorialized and buried. When parents leave specific directions or have shared their wishes, this task is fairly straightforward. But it is not always so simple.
>
> Planning a funeral can be a formidable responsibility, especially for an adult child who has never dealt directly with death. Some individuals are too overwhelmed to make these kinds of decisions. The pressure is tremendous because

decisions must be made quickly. For others, planning the funeral or memorial rites for our last parent is a positive experience, albeit sorrowful, for it enables us to feel very adult and to repay our parents for all that they did for us.[10]

Sibling Rivalry at This Age?

If you have siblings, it's important to remember that each child has a different relationship with the same set of parents. Each will have different memories and experiences as well as different degrees of closeness with the deceased. You may have a discussion with one sibling about your parents and end up thinking, *That wasn't the mother or father I grew up with!*

When your parents die, interaction with siblings becomes a necessity. But siblings come in all sizes and personalities and histories. You may either have positive experiences with them or would rather avoid them. The differences, rivalries and arguments of the past may rise again, especially when you have to make final arrangements and decide what to do with your parent's property. And what if there's more than one family involved? When there has been a remarriage and blending of two families, there can be major complications.

Were you and your siblings close? Are you in agreement over the final arrangements, or is there tension? Some families develop a closeness while others are fragmented. What will you do with your parent's legacy? As Jane Brooks states:

> When sibling relationships are strong, there is likely to be very little change after the death of the last parent. If anything, sisters and brothers who have been close are drawn even closer in their mutual loss. Sometimes, when siblings have not been particularly close or are even estranged, the death of the last parent cements a relationship as the family pulls itself together. However, a wobbly relationship is just as apt to fall apart when there are no longer parents to pull the siblings together. The catalyst for the final blow to an ailing

relationship is often the division of parents' personal property.

On the surface, this job is nothing more than a practical matter—"you get this, I get that." In reality, though, the division of our parent's property is a rite of passage laden with potentially wrenching emotional and psychological issues. Watching our parents get sick and die depletes us emotionally. Planning the funeral is wrenching. But it is the experience of settling the estate that brings us face-to-face with our new status in the family album, and it can take its toll as family dynamics shift. For many of us, the experience itself is bittersweet as we are suddenly handed what took our parents a lifetime to accumulate.

When parents played favorites with the children, possessions take on a symbolic value. If the sibling perceived as the "favorite" gets more of the goods, then the other sibling interprets that as a sign of less parental love. The "loser" turns his or her rage on the sibling, who always did and even now "gets it all."

Without parents to intervene, it falls on us to negotiate our way through this process with our siblings. How we handle this significant rite of passage can have an enduring effect on the next stage of our lives.[11]

Record a Written History

With the loss of your parent, at some point in time, and when you're ready, writing a relationship review may be helpful. This can take any form you wish. It's often not helpful to write it out longhand. Describe your parent as you remember him or her. Describe him or her when you were a child, a young adult and now. Then write how this parent would describe you at these same times of your life. How would you describe the relationship you had with your parent? What did you do together?

My mother died at 93, and for her last 15 years she lived close to us in a retirement community. I called her every day during the last 10 years of her life, and we talked for perhaps five minutes each time. I knew in advance what we would talk about, but we made contact each day. Every Wednesday evening I took her out to dinner. It was our family ritual. As I wrote this section, I happened to find a picture of her and me together at dinner, which elicited some positive memories and brought back a sense of gladness for the time we spent together.

What about you? What did you do together? Where did you go, and what did you do? What did you talk about? What did you agree or disagree about? How would your parent respond to these questions? What were significant events in your life with this parent? What do you wish could have been different? What might your parent have wished could have been different about you?

Make a list of the questions you wish you could have asked this parent. Is there anyone in the family who could answer these questions for you?

Have you created a written history of your parents' lives? This is one way to make sure your parents are not forgotten and their history can be passed on to the next generation. As you look through their records or letters, you may discover items and information you weren't ever aware of until now. Saving the sympathy cards and notes are important, for often they provide you with information about your parents that others have and you may not. These help you see your parent as an individual and not just as mother or father.

Take a Personal Survey

How are you doing with your grief at this time? Consider these questions. They may or may not apply to you.
- Are you still struggling with accepting that your mother and/or father is dead, even though it's been some time? Are you expecting them to return? Is it time to move some things out of where they lived if your other parent is still there?
- Have you isolated yourself from friends or relatives for a long period of time? Are you concerned about

what is occurring in their lives or have any desire to see them?
- What did you used to do that you no longer have any interest in? How long has this gone on?
- How are you doing in taking care of your basic needs? What isn't being taken care of at this time, and how long has this gone on?
- What's the status of your health? Has there been any deterioration in any way? When is the last time you had a complete physical?
- Are you dependent on alcohol or drugs, or do you use these to deaden the pain of your loss?
- On a scale of 0 to 10, how concerned are you about your own progress in the grief journey?[12]

In the next chapter, we will focus on your specific relationship as a daughter or son and those unique dynamics.

6

Parent Loss—A Woman and Her Mother; A Man and His Father

The death of a parent at any time is a major loss to a child. It changes your life in so many ways and brings with it the loss of certain hopes and dreams. Not only can it be the death of part of your past, but it can also be the death of part of the present and future as well.

A Woman's Loss of Her Mother

If you are a woman and your past with your mother was lacking, you may have been looking forward to a new future with her. But that is gone. Perhaps you had a list of questions to ask or grievances to share or a confrontation you had waited years to express. That opportunity is lost along with your mother.

Your identity undergoes a change, and in a way you feel orphaned. Your sense of loss is affected by your mother's spiritual condition as well—was she or wasn't she a believer? If your mother died at a middle age, you also end up mourning the opportunities you feel she lost, for the years she would never live and the dreams she would never fulfill. Her death can lead you to question what her life was for and what it meant.

The early death of a mother robs a daughter of memories. As a result, she sometimes makes up her own memories, which often idealize her mother. Daughters who lose their mothers to early death are frozen in time. They had no chance to see their mother grow and change or display weaknesses or strengths. In other words, they didn't see their mother as a real person, so they invented in their minds the mother they wanted to have.

Author Therese Rando had this insightful comment on the death of a parent:

> Like a community or institution that loses its archives in a fire, we have been stripped of a form of documentation of our lives and our history. We also have lost the direct links to our past and to unremembered parts of ourselves....[1]

When a mother dies something else also dies—the buffer between you and death. Keep in mind if both of your parents died, you have now become the older generation. There's no generation in front of you to insulate you. You're much more aware of your mortality....[2]

There's another change as well, "With the death of your parent you lose opportunities to atone or make up for unpleasantness in the past or to have further contact in the future. Along with this you may feel quite grieved over the fact that you couldn't have helped your parent in the way you would have liked. You may recall how this person always would help you out, how she constantly took care of you first before herself, how she could always fix what was wrong. Now you are in a position where you would want to return the favors to help. To take care of, to correct so she doesn't have to die. Your sadness and frustration at not being able to make it 'all better' ... can be powerful."[3]

What is it like to lose your mother? One woman described it this way: "I can no longer hear her voice, as hard as I try. I would give so much to hear her say my name again."

Hope Edelman suggests that grieving over a mother never disappears for good. She says, "When you lose a mother, the intervals between grief responses lengthen over time, but the longing never disappears. It always hovers at the edge of your awareness, prepared to surface at any time, in any place, in the least expected ways. Despite popular belief to the contrary, this isn't pathological; it's normal. And it's why you find yourself at 24 or 35 or 43 unwrapping a present or walking down an aisle or crossing a busy street doubled over and missing your mother because she died when you were seventeen."[4]

Patricia Commins states in *Remembering Mother, Finding Myself:*

> When it comes to our relationships with our deceased mothers, many of us are locked in an emotional time warp. Regardless of how far we've come in other areas of our lives, personal or professional, our relationships with our mothers are the same now as they were at the time of our mother's death.
>
> A daughter's attitude toward her mother's death, says Dr. Joyce Fraser, a psychologist in St. Claire Shores, Michigan, reflects where she is emotionally at that time in her life. Daughters who are "less involved" in their relationships with their mothers see the world through the "prism of their own needs," she adds. Often these daughters are very angry over their mothers' deaths, which they may view as abandonment. "Who is going to take

care of me?" they ask themselves and the world. "Why did you leave me?" In a more evolved mother-daughter relationship, the death is viewed more as a natural part of the life cycle, even though these daughters still grieve the loss.

Unless we work on issues with our mothers that remain after their deaths, we can be trapped in an emotional suspended animation.[5]

In *Losing a Parent,* Fiona Marshall states that a parent's death may seem like the beginning of your own death—the first pull of yourself toward that great darkness. It strikes home with real force: "If they can die, then so can I!" You have to work through the implications of this for a long time during bereavement.[6]

If a mother dies of a long-term illness, other losses were probably experienced along the way, such as the other parent's attention and involvement, financial adjustments, the family's way of life, and so on. Perhaps you had to function as a caregiver. And how the mother handles the illness, as well as facing her death, influences you.

If the death was from a long-term illness, much of the grieving occurs prior to the death, which allows you to give up dreams and expectations for the relationship with your parent, piece by piece. Author Harold Ivan Smith states:

> Some mothers served as the glue that held a fragile family together. Some of us grieve for a mother *and* for a family that disintegrated after death. Some siblings have been on their best behavior while their mother was dying. Nothing—including family dysfunction—was allowed to upset Mother. That fragile truce continued in some families through the rituals; in others, all it took to unravel was divvying up Mom's estate. A punch bowl can become a battleground that resurrects old family issues. The family has never been the same—and never will be. Family histories may be divided BMD and AMD: *before* Mom's death and *after* Mom's death....[7] A mother's death can make shambles of schedules, priorities, agendas, commitments—sometimes, our most

intimate relationships. A mother's last breath inevitably changes us. Motherlessness can be paralyzing or it can be empowering. It can cause us to take life far more seriously.[8]

In *Losing a Parent,* Fiona Marshall states:

> Sudden death is more often heard than witnessed. Because of this, you may feel anguish, wondering what your mother's last moments were like, whether they were terrifying or painful.
>
> It is natural for their seconds or minutes of dying to become your hours of emotional distress. Turning off your thoughts by sheer willpower alone is not easy and often impossible. At some point, you may need to talk to someone.
>
> The fact that you weren't there when she died can also be a source of long-lasting regret. The fact that *no one* may have been there can also be stressful. You may have to deal with the length of a painful mental process of second-guessing, *if only* your mother had consulted

a doctor earlier, and so on. Sudden deaths are often bizarre, like nightmares, because they are so unexpected. This is especially true when they are accidents....[9]

To some extent, it is possible to experience survivor guilt after any death, even if the death wasn't part of some disaster. Why should we still be alive when someone else has died?

If only you had called the ambulance an hour earlier, *if only* you had persuaded Mom to give up her job last year. Surely there must have been something you could have done?

Survivor guilt deals with the fact that we still consider ourselves responsible and powerful in the face of death, even though all the evidence proves otherwise. When we're used to making life better by our own efforts, it's hard to let go and admit there was absolutely nothing we could do.

Linked to this is a certain uneasy feeling that our own need to live somehow contributed to our parent's death.

The fact that a parent's death removes the buffering generation between ourselves and death can also mean that guilt blends into fear. Thoughts of "it might be me next" or "it could have been me" are common.

You may have to come to terms with guilt over "not being good enough" as a child. The child's self-centeredness can be profound—that feeling that you're somehow responsible for everything.[10]

With a sudden death, you end up feeling helpless and powerless. You feel confused over what happened and can have feelings of regret and guilt even months or years later. For this reason, it's important to return as objectively as possible to the event and consider several questions.[11] In regard to your mother's death:

What were you able to do?

_____

_____

_____

What were you unable to do?
_____
_____

What were others unable to do?
_____
_____

What made you feel that you were able to help?
_____
_____

What made you feel powerless to help?
_____
_____

What do you now realize about the situation?
_____
_____

What do you miss most about her now?
_____
_____

Even when a daughter carries painful memories of her relationship with her mother, death carries a sting. It signifies an end to those intense years that have taken such a toll in her life. The events themselves can never be forgotten, but the pain of the memories must be dealt with or they can keep a daughter snared by unhappiness. We can choose to bring the pain of the past along with our loved ones.[12]

When a mother dies, one of the most common issues is the goodbyes that were said or not said. Sometimes goodbyes are verbal, while others are nonverbal. How did your mother say goodbye? If she didn't, or was unable to, how might she have said it? Describe how you would have liked her to say goodbye to you and how you would have liked to say goodbye to your mother.

It is still possible for this to occur. You can write your mother a detailed goodbye letter and read it out loud either at the gravesite or to an empty chair. Some have a gathering of friends at a "goodbye gathering" similar to a memorial service.

Sometimes after a mother's death, a daughter sees her mother more as she has really been—she loses both a person and, at the same time, discovers someone. Given this, what do you know about your mother?

What I know about my mother's childhood:

___

___

What I know about my mother's adolescence:

___

___

When she was young she wanted to be:

___

___

My mother accomplished:

___

___

What she liked was:

___

___

What she loved was:
_____
_____

Those she was closest to were:
_____
_____

My mother's relationship with her mother was:
_____
_____

Mother was happiest when:
_____
_____

A Man's Loss of His Father

When a man experiences the death of his father, it can be overwhelming for many reasons. Loss by death is enough in itself, but most of us don't know how to grieve. My father was killed in an automobile accident when I was 22. The notification came from my uncle over the phone, "Your dad was killed in a car wreck on the way home." It felt like my world had collapsed.

My first major death. After I wept, I busied myself. I didn't know what else to do. It was my mom's second tragic loss of a husband, and I didn't know what to say to her or what to do for her. I went back to graduate school two days later.

Men are expected to quickly bounce back to everyday life. My stepson lost his father just two days before I wrote this section. His place of employment gave him one day off for bereavement and then expected him back to work.

Most men are concerned about doing what is right in grief even when we don't know what is right to begin with. If the pain is too much, we look for ways to numb the pain.

In our culture, fathers are usually the first to die in a family. This impacts a man more than he realizes. Lee Hough, a friend of mine, once said:

> The death of a father, yours, mine, everyone's, is traumatic, especially since it is often the first loss of a parent that a son experiences. The very man who

gave us life, held us, fed us, steadied our bikes, cheered us on the field, modeled for us in the home, counseled us in our careers, and hugged us in our tears—when he dies, when we must watch him die, a part of us dies as well. No matter how well adjusted or strong we are, each son experiences the Super Bowl of grief. It is at this time when another coach and mentor is desperately needed—someone to lead us through this most painful rite of passage.[13]

The resemblance of a son to his father is another element that impacts many men. When they hear, "You're just like your dad," it's like dad was a reflective mirror. Many men identify so much with their dad that when he dies, the son feels that part of him died as well. Because of this closeness, even though a man's mother is still living, he often feels like an orphan.

Most of us live as though we're invincible. The truth that we're not hits us when our father dies. We realize that it's just the opposite—life is terminal, death is real, not for someone else but for us as well. Most men live with the illusion of always being in control of their own life—that we can predict and be in charge of our future. A father's death brings home in a very intense manner that control is an illusion. As one author described what happens: "Grief is the great emasculator. Most of us will know no other time in our lives when we have been so absolutely and completely stripped of control; this insecurity is especially intense for men whose identity, worth and self-esteem are tied closely to issues of power and authority."[14]

Realizing that life is brief can help us value each moment in a new way. In the Bible, David expressed it this way:

> LORD, remind me how brief my time on earth will be.
> Remind me that my days are numbered—
> how fleeting my life is.
>
> You have made my life no longer than the width of my hand.

> My entire lifetime is just a moment to you;
> at best, each of us is but a breath.
> And so, Lord, where do I put my hope?
> My only hope is in you (Ps. 39:4-5,7, *NLT*).

> So teach us to number our days,
> That we may present to You a heart of wisdom
> (Ps. 90:12, *NASB*).

For many men, the death of their father is the death of their cheering section. Their dad was their guidance. His death means losing someone who gave affirmation and approval. For others who never had a positive relationship with their dad, it's like a door has permanently slammed shut. The opportunity of perhaps building a positive relationship, of healing and reconciliation, has been taken away. And so it's not just the loss of a person but of opportunities as well. These losses leave a feeling of unfinished business, which can create anger and/or regret. John Trent described this as follows:

> For me, my father really died twice.
>
> I grew up without a father. Dad divorced Mom when I was two-and-a-half months old, so I didn't know him and, in fact, didn't even meet him until I was a teenager. So I went from being a toddler and knowing no father, to a young child in grade school asking questions about my father, and even into high school without knowing him. Then all of a sudden I met him. The sad part (I detail this in *Choosing to Live the Blessing*) came when he said he wanted to see me play football. Our team was doing pretty well, and the local paper had a story about the team, with a picture of my twin brother and me. My father read the paper and actually called my mom and asked if he could come to the game. My brother and I played our hearts out that night, thinking he was in the stands, and expected to see him after the game, but he

never showed up and never even bothered to call to say he wasn't coming. So, for me, my father died that day because I experienced the death of a dream.

Dad died, again, on August 6, about six years ago.[15]

What were the losses you experienced from the death of your father?

_____

_____

_____

A father's death for a son can have many effects. He could become more responsible, more motivated to be a man of integrity, to grow more spiritually, to bring siblings closer together, to work harder, to care for those remaining members of the family. When a father's chair sits empty, a son could realize for the first time that he will be filling it. As Dave Veerman and Bruce Barton state:

> Some men described the feeling [of a father's passing] as one of being delegated new responsibilities and authority. [One man] reflects this when he says, "I felt that a

page had been turned in my life, and the cycle was complete. The 'baton' had been passed to me. I no longer could be considered the son. I was now fully the father and had to take on the mantle that the title held. I don't think my behavior changed much, but the emotion did change. It was a sad feeling but a necessary passage for me."[16]

Dr. Paul Thigpen wrote the following, which he titled "To My Father on the First Anniversary of His Passing":

> A year ago today I stood and wept beside your bed.
> The veil was rent, and through the tear I caught a glimpse of glory;
> I saw you crush the mocking Serpent underneath your heel.
> I saw you drop the weary rags and don the shining robe.
> I saw you laugh at fear and trade your trial for a crown.
> I saw you greet the Shepherd and lie down beside His stream.
> So many gifts you gave me, but the last by far was best;
> A year ago, on your deathbed, your son was new-begotten.

My grief gave way to courage then and I became a man.[17]

In *Lessons from a Father to a Son,* John Ashcroft states, "It has been said that a man is not a man until his father is gone. If this was what manhood felt like, I had real questions about whether I was up to it."[18]

When a father dies, it doesn't mean he's gone. Many of his possessions will remain with you. In fact, you may struggle with what to keep and what to discard. If something was of value to your dad, it may now have increased value for you because it's your last connection. My dad died more than 50 years ago, but I still have the box with several items that were his. I don't intend to discard them even though I don't have any use for most of them. One man described the connection: "Every time I make a cast with his fly rod and one of his flies I'm reminded of him and what we shared together."

Sometimes after a father's death you want to revisit certain places that were special for the two of you. If you want to do this, others don't have to understand why it's important to you. Your memories help you rethink your life and what you want to do with it at this time.[19]

In a major loss such as any family death, it is often difficult to take action because most of the "action" activities related to the loss are "subcontracted." Think about it—what is there *to do?* The "death professionals" take charge—building and providing the coffin, organizing the service, digging the grave, obtaining the flowers and even driving to the funeral. It is difficult for us as men to stand around and have nothing to do when the opportunity for activity has been taken away.

For some, rigorous physical activity can result in healing. The need to engage in such activities produces unique responses as various personalities try to cope with loss. I heard about a man who had lost his father in a tragic fire. He lived near his father on an adjacent farm. One night the home in which he was born and raised burned to the ground, and his father was inside. The man's response to this tragedy startled other family members. He remained silent while they wept and talked about the loss.

After a rain had extinguished the fire, the man borrowed a bulldozer and proceeded to bulldoze the ashes and charred remains of the house. This action was how he expressed his need to bury his father. He worked for hours, not stopping for meals or rest. When darkness fell, he continued, ignoring the requests of family members to stop for the night. He continued to bulldoze the remains back and forth, again and again.

This man and his father were farmers, and for most of their lives had worked together in the fields. They didn't verbalize much together nor share feelings; but they had a close, nonverbal relationship.

Some may grieve with tears, but this man grieved with a borrowed bulldozer. Taking this kind of action was his own personal expression of words and tears. He "cried" by working the land over and over again until nothing was visible. He gave his father and the home a proper burial, but in his own way. The land, which in a sense was his father's cemetery, was not ready to be farmed—and the son would be the one to do it. If you were to ask this man why he had done this, he could not give you an answer. He didn't want to know why, but he did something with his grief, and it was probably the best thing he could have done.[20] What will you do? What can you do?

It's interesting to note both the differences and similarities in the way men act out their grief in various cultures.

In some societies, such as the Bara people in Madagascar, men and women actually separate from each other following a death. A "male hut" is designated for men, and a "house of tears" for women. The latter is the place of emotional expression, but the male house is the center of action where the men work out the details of the funeral ritual.

Other cultures actually give men active tasks. In Nigeria, the Dagura men dance out the life of the person who died. Other cultures have the men sing about the life of the dead person.[21]

For some of us, just doing something—anything—is a way of grieving. As a wife in counseling expressed it, "It's like he is on a treadmill. I wish he would sit for a while. He just goes and goes and goes. And when I suggest that he cut back, he says it hurts too much when he does nothing."

When the news of a serious loss first hits us, we may throw ourselves with fervor into work and household activity in an attempt to overcome the feelings of powerlessness and pain. Our hours at work may increase, or we may become obsessive in fixing up the house. The increased activity is noticeable to others by its intensity.

Another male response can be expected when we suffer a significant loss. We tend to do everything possible *not* to show our fear or insecurity. We men don't do well admitting our fears.

Years ago, I learned to ask my counselees (male and female), "What is the fear in your life that drives you?" I was amazed at the extent of fear I uncovered. Most of us are more driven by fear than drawn by hope. Our behavior certainly doesn't reflect fear, but often it could be prompted by fear.

One of a man's common fears is: *If I show despair or depression, how do I know that eventually I'll be okay? What will keep it from going on and on?* I like what I hear in this message from a grief therapist to a grieving man:

> If you are among those who feel that you do not know how intense, lengthy or deep your expression of grief may be, you may find yourself thinking that it would be impossible—or at least very difficult for you to pull out of grief's deep pit to do all the things you need to do before or after the death. Being afraid of getting sucked down into a hollow of "no return" is not realistic. *Grief is not quicksand. Rather, it is a walk on rocky terrain that eventually smoothes out and proves less challenging—both emotionally and physically.* So if you find yourself fearful and grieving, if you're imagining the worst or expecting some untenable transformation to take place within

yourself, try putting those catastrophic thoughts in their proper perspective.

For example, you may think: *I will fall apart and won't be able to function if I start to show how I feel.* Replace such a thought with the more realistic: I will let go for a time, release what I feel, and will be able to function better as a result of having vented the feelings that are an ever-present burden.

You may think: *If I let myself, then I will change permanently and won't ever be able to be myself again.* It's a fact that grief changes most survivors whether or not they vent their emotions and express their feelings. You can't keep change from happening after a loss; it is part of surviving a death. But you can take control over the type of change you experience. As you allow yourself to grieve, the changes that take place will be ones which allow you to go forward, to integrate loss, and to resolve the issues related to your loved one's death. Venting your responses can be like turning a searchlight on something moving in the shadows—which you imagine to be more enormous and menacing than it really is. Once the light is on, your caution seems to have been completely unnecessary.[22]

7

The Loss of a Sibling

The loss of your sibling is made even more painful because you're often a "forgotten griever." There are other names for those who have lost a sibling, such as the "lonely griever." There is no other loss in childhood or adulthood that seems to be so neglected as the death of a brother or a sister. Often we have several siblings, and thus we are more exposed to the death of a sibling than to other deaths.

My mother experienced the loss of all six of her siblings before she died. There's an assumption that the loss of a parent or a spouse is the most distressing, but for some adults, sibling loss is the hardest.

John had two brothers—one was two years older, and one was two years younger. When his older brother died, he lost someone who had been a part of his life from the very beginning. In some ways, siblings define us. We become "John's brother" or "Sue's sister." It's common for a sibling to explain himself in relationship to a deceased sibling: "I act like my dad and Sam was more like mom."[1] John's future with this brother was gone. No longer would they share the memories, family traditions or birthdays. A constant was gone from John's life. His brother's death made him feel older and much more mortal. His family of origin had shrunk by one-third. He found himself wondering if he, too, would die when he reached his brother's age. The bell that tolls for a sibling may keep on tolling with the message, "You're next."

When a sibling dies, very few take into account the depth of the bond that can occur between two siblings. If you've lost an adult sibling, you may have heard insensitive responses such as, "Just be glad it wasn't your child or your spouse." It's as though the death of a sibling is dismissed, since a brother or sister is not considered one of the central characters of your life. So, in addition to losing your sibling, you lose the support of others during your grief. This could include your own spouse and children since they didn't have the same relationship with your sibling as you did. Indeed, you do feel like a lonely mourner.[2]

Why Sibling Loss Is So Significant

Your relationship with your brothers and sisters are key to understanding yourself. Where they end and where you begin is often so seamless that the loss of a sibling can be a crippling blow to your understanding of who you are and how you function and relate to others. I suspect this holds true even in cases in which people have distant or troubled relationships with their brothers and sisters. "Closeness" is not, as we often presume, a prerequisite for connection, and the story of "intimate" relationship is not always a happy one.

I've come to think of siblings as an actor might think of a back-story—the imagined background of a character he's going to play. Those of us in the audience may never get a glimmer of a character's imagined history, but it's there all the same, informing that character's identity, behavior and choices. Those of us who have siblings all have a backstory.

It is, therefore, all the more perplexing that the loss of a sibling has been considered less significant than other losses.

Siblings have influenced and shaped our lives more than we ever realize. We don't remember many of our early experiences. We don't have the language for their recall when we're so young. But our early experiences are really the foundation of our world today. The author of *The Empty Room* describes the influences of a sibling:

> We remember some of the events of childhood, the bigger events that are most often witnessed by others and tend to become the stuff of family stories. It's the day-to-day moments and the things you yourself can't remember that constitute the true basis of the relationship.
>
> It's a process of hardwiring, learning the world with someone by your side as witness, peer, protector, antagonist or all of the above. It is what makes you know,

at a later date, when your mind is sufficiently developed to wonder about such things, that these people are intimately, sometimes even uncomfortably, connected to you without being able to articulate in any convincing manner, to yourself or others, exactly how or why. At some point in time (a time that most of us won't remember) siblings become interstitial: lodged between your cells. They are the invisible glue that holds your interior architecture together.[3]

Adults usually grieve deeply when they lose a sibling. You may have shared life with him or her for most of your existence. I've heard a number of adults say, "I just can't remember life without them. There's a giant hole there."

No One Else Can Fill His or Her Shoes

When your sibling died, you lost more than that person. You lost his or her role within the family. What he or she did is gone, and that is disruptive.

There are many roles to be played out within a family structure, and siblings play a number of roles.
- *The Mediator:* A family usually has a mediator, an individual everyone turns to when a problem needs to be settled. Others see him or her as the person who is fair. This individual is a problem solver.
- *The Entertainer:* Some siblings serve in the role of entertainer. It's as if they barge into the room with a dramatic flair, singing, "Let me entertain you." Entertainers orchestrate the family's social life, including where, when and how. They are the family's link to the outside world because of their contacts with others.
- *The Enabler:* Enablers provide emotional and relational nurture and a sense of belonging. Since they usually want to preserve the family unity at all costs, they often go to extremes to keep the peace. Their goal is to eliminate all conflicts and to help everyone get along. Unfortunately, with an enabler in control, conflicts are more often

buried and perpetuated rather than resolved.

- *The Doer:* The doer in your family was the one who said, "Give it to me and it will get done." Doers have an overdeveloped sense of responsibility that often drives them unmercifully. They provide most of the maintenance functions in a family. Doers also are referred to as the responsible ones. We usually remember the doers in our family of origin because they always took up the slack. Who assumed this role in your growing-up years?
- *Heroes and Caretakers.* Heroes can be doers or caretakers. A hero's success and achievement bring recognition and prestige to the family. A hero becomes addicted to pleasing others. Sometimes the hero fulfills the family dream, adopting it as his or her own. The esteem the hero receives builds up the rest of the family. Remember, a caretaker or hero is an overly responsible person.
- *The Clown:* The family clown brings humor into the family through play,

and even silliness. The clowns are always joking and cutting up, especially when confronted by difficult situations. Their funny nature is a great cover-up for any deep pain or isolation. Humor brings the attention clowns may feel unable to merit in other areas.
- *The Manipulator:* Manipulators are the clever controllers in the family who learned early on how to get others to do what they wanted. They know how to seduce, charm, play sick or appear weak. They can and often do use every trick in the book to get their way.
- *The Critic:* Critics are the faultfinding negativists who always see the glass as half empty instead of half full. Sarcasm, hurtful teasing and complaining characterize the Critic's behavior. They prefer to use their energy to tear others down rather than build them up. Critics are not very pleasant to be around, but some families end up enduring them.
- *The Scapegoat:* Scapegoats are the victims who actually end up as the family-blame collectors. The victim's

misbehavior makes everyone else's behavior look good, causing the rest of them to think that if it weren't for the scapegoat, the family would be just about perfect.

Each role fulfills a specialized function within the family, and the scapegoat is not exceptional.

So, who will fill in for that brother or sister? Maybe your family role was tied into your birth order. If your sibling was the oldest, you may have lost a caregiver or protector or someone you looked up to. If he or she was much older, you may feel as though you lost a parent; or if he or she was younger, you lost a child.

With the death of a sibling, there's a gap in the birth order. If there were just two of you, you're now an only child. If you were a twin, it's normal to feel that part of you died as well.

Family Connections Get Reshuffled

For some, the death may alter your relationship with your parents in some way, both from your part as well as theirs. They may try to comfort you at the expense of themselves, or protect you, or you may try to do the same. Part of the difficulty may be due to lack of knowledge about the grieving process.

You will still have a relationship with your sibling's family, and they will serve as reminders—the special moments in your nieces' or nephews' lives may be difficult as well as a delight, and they may need you to share your repertoire of memories.

Even though this was the loss of your sibling, it's still a loss for your family members too. They will need support and comfort. When a sibling dies, you're likely to become so much more aware of your own mortality. It could have been you who died.

If a sibling had a terminal illness, others may experience old rivalries at this time. Attention and financial resources of parents and others are directed toward that sibling. This and other issues can generate resentment, which may later come back to haunt you after your sibling dies. The obvious door to guilt opens wide.

Old Rivalries Rise Again

There are other issues to consider as well. What if you were still caught up in sibling rivalry? This could feed guilt feelings as well as regrets. Perhaps part of you experiences some relief that some of your lifelong hassles are now gone. These are normal thoughts and feelings.

Just as guilt can come to a child who loses a sibling, it can come to you, perhaps for different reasons. It may begin with remembering how close you were when you were younger. Then you begin wishing you had done more to perpetuate that closeness, but you didn't, and now it's too late. Or maybe there were unresolved issues that you now wish had been settled. Perhaps you wonder why your sibling died first, which activates survivor guilt. All of these feelings may be compounded with the additional loss of not being included in decisions about the funeral arrangements because all of that was left to the surviving spouse and children.

Over the years, I have seen numerous wars, not so much between nations or between parents and children, but ongoing wars between siblings. Some of these wars have lasted for more than a quarter of a century. The weapons used included bickering, hateful comments, spiteful letters, hung-up phone calls, not talking or seeing one another for years and even permanent separation. Siblings lose one another in death, but in some ways it's worse when the loss is by conflict.

All siblings disagree, fight and compete as children. You probably did. What were your fights about? Was it to gain power and control over a brother or sister? Could it have been a desire to have more attention or a better position with your parents? Or perhaps it was over territory, toys, other possessions, friends or a desire to goad your brother or sister into a reaction. Were these fights always negative and harmful? Probably not. They had a purpose, part of which was to educate and prepare you for life.

Even though the battles were painful at times, they helped you come to understand your own strengths and limitations. You learned to assess your ability to bargain, negotiate or handle conflict and anger, all of which you would need as you grew older. You possibly found out about loyalty, fairness and trust. You learned that it was all right to disagree, to have different points of view, that as different as you and your sibling are, it was all right for you to be you and for him or her to be whoever he or she was. And, hopefully, you learned how to resolve differences, so that you could respond differently the next time. You may not have liked the hassling, but having experienced it, you are better off and better prepared for life than those who grew up without it. This experience helped you to relate and connect better in your adult world.

When you disagree with a sibling, as compared to a friend, you probably are more blunt and honest. You usually don't hold back. Why? Because you feel more secure with family members than with friends. The relationship had a greater sense of permanency, despite differences.

The fighting and squabbling of childhood normally diminishes in adulthood—at least, for most it does. For others, the ongoing battle continues. It may be a continuation of the same issues of childhood, or it could be the same themes but with different packaging. Almost every phone call or get-together can be a continuation of where the last phone call or visit left off without a break since childhood.

What if your relationship with your siblings wasn't all that it could have been, and conflict was the common denominator? Perhaps you believed that someday you would build a positive relationship, and now someday is just a vapor and an unfulfilled dream. Many carry the residue of guilt after the death of a brother or sister. What can you do to move forward in a positive way?

Accentuate the Good

If you could have the opportunity to sit down with your sibling and discuss your issues and share what you regret and what you wish you could have together, what would you say? You can still do this by writing a letter (in longhand), expressing in detail your thoughts and feelings. Read it aloud to an empty chair, a trusted friend or a counselor.

It's easy to focus on what was negative or painful or lacking, but this often overlooks the other side.

Since your brother or sister isn't alive, you can't change the unchangeable. You can't change what occurred in the past, but you can change your response to it. Many have found it helpful to focus on the positive elements that were present. What was the good, the positive, the shared special times together? Some have found it helpful to create some type of a positive, lasting memorial. One creative approach is to create a sibling storybook—a history of you and your sibling that you could share with others. Or it could just be one positive or funny incident rather than an entire story. Photographs or other keepsakes could be a part of this.

Another possibility is more of a ritual called a healing ceremony. It's a way of facing the guilt and regrets of the past and letting them go. You could listen to music, read from the psalms and then participate in a hand-washing ceremony, signifying the washing away of guilt and regret. Some express their feelings out loud to the person while pouring the water over their hands. Others catch the water in a bowl, place it in a vial and then pour it out into a lake or stream or ocean. These are steps you can take to reduce the pain of the past and move forward.

Positive Ways to Deal with Accumulated Losses

One of your other concerns may be the family members whom your sibling left. Some of them you may like and others you may dislike. Some you would like to continue to see, while it's more of a relief not to be in the life of others. Perhaps your sibling's spouse begins to date, remarries and then moves across the country. Your losses are beginning to accumulate.[4]

Because of this death, your relationship with other family members will also die in one sense. Roles change.

It usually changes with your parents. You may find that some distance begins to occur between you and your parents. One of you may engage in long-term thinking while the other finds it overwhelming to just get through each day.

If your parents begin to idealize your sibling, you may end up with an abundance of pain. Your parents are seeing what they want to see. This may be difficult to handle since your relationship with your sibling was different, and you had access to information about him or her that was unknown to your parents. Out of respect you didn't say anything. Often parents focus on the strengths and joys, and you wonder where you stand in all of this. Grief can exaggerate positive and negative feelings between you and the deceased.[5]

A number of individuals wonder about the sibling rivalry that existed. It's a natural part of growing up, and in some families it isn't even witnessed by others because it's minimal. Some struggle with guilt over this and even blow it out of proportion. Don't focus on or magnify regrets. For each rivalry you dwell on, counter it with a positive memory. Pamela Blair and Brook Noel wrote:

> Siblings often have a love-hate relationship until well into adulthood. When we're still kids, it's not uncommon to be best friends one minute and worst enemies the next. This double-sided relationship often complicates the grief process. You will find yourself wishing you had been nicer, more forgiving, or less jealous. Blame and guilt can reign strong for surviving children. Grief exaggerates both the positive and the negative of any relationships. Because the relationship can no longer evolve or change, it's frozen in time, and we tend to hone in on specific moments in a way we would not do with those who are living. Relationships are not comprised by one-time moments but rather by a garland of moments over time. If we pick out specific moments, we disrupt the entire garland. Focus on

the whole and not the individual parts.[6]

The loss of your brother or sister may create difficult issues in your own family. Your family had a different relationship with your sibling and may not be as supportive as you want, for they don't understand the impact. You need someone to share your emotions with.

Several factors impact your life. What was the intensity of the death? If you actually see a brother or sister die, it may bring on a lasting trauma. The event may always be remembered but not talked about, whether it is witnessing an accident or observing the last moments of a sibling's life on a deathbed. Consider the impact of discovering your sibling floating facedown in a swimming pool or seeing him or her struck by a car.

But even if the death occurred elsewhere, and you learned of it secondhand, there still are problems. What actually happened to your sibling is left to your imagination, particularly if there is no opportunity to view the body. This could lead to a denial of the loss.

A common feeling is that you could have done something to prevent the loss. You may feel that you somehow caused your sibling's death. In the 1980 film *Ordinary People,* Conrad Jarrett could never be sure that he had done all he could to save his older brother from drowning. Many struggle with the thought that their sibling's death might have been prevented.

It's been said that there is no other loss in our adult life that is so neglected, even though most of us will experience it at some time. In fact, sibling losses may outnumber any other losses.

If you were close in age to your sibling when he or she died, you will experience many of the same losses as if this event had occurred in childhood. One of the features of sibling death, and one you need to expect, is that there will be less social recognition of the significance of this loss. The loss may not have the same impact on other family members of your immediate family as it does on you. If you have other siblings, they may respond quite differently to the loss than you do.

With a sibling gone, the roles and relationships with other family members may need to undergo a change. This, too, may entail more loss and stress, as it did in Ted's case. Ted was the second of two sons, and he lived in the shadow of his older brother. After his brother died, he received more attention and recognition for his achievements, but he also had to assume his deceased brother's role of being responsible for his elderly parents.[7] What is your role?

Remember that the other siblings who are living may not have the same connection with the deceased sibling as you did. You have a unique co-history with your sibling. This person you lost took with him or her one of your main connections with the past; your sibling knew you in a special way and you knew him or her in a special way.

There may have been issues or situations that either brought you closer together over the years or drove you apart. Perhaps you've experienced some of the following situations.

A sibling lost his or her spouse and became more dependent on you for an extended period of time, either emotionally or financially.

Perhaps one of you received a promotion or transfer and moved away for the first time.

Or one sibling couldn't have children and the others did.

One loses a job and has financial pressures, looking either to you or your parents for help. Perhaps one has to move into your parents' home and disrupts their lives by needing them to baby-sit.

Other issues could include not having much say in the final preparations for the service and burial. Or you're not asked to say anything at the services, and yet you have more history with the deceased than his or her spouse or children.

You may find yourself continuing to react as though your sibling were still here as you plan your weekly luncheon or phone calls or find yourself texting, and no one responds. Perhaps your sibling's voice was on the answering machine and now it's been erased.

Many of your concerns are similar to a parent's when his or her adult child dies. How will your sibling's children get along, and who will influence them like your brother or sister did? What if your in-law begins to date, and what if you lose contact with your niece or nephew?[8]

Perhaps the various aspects of losing a sibling as an adult can best be described by a woman who lost her younger brother:

> I grieved now for Bob, my brother, who was not only a member of my family but someone who knew me, who understood me, who felt with me, in a way no one else on this planet ever did or would. Someone who, more than I had ever dared know, was me. My brother-double.
>
> And I grieved, too, still more deeply, for all that now would never be. For except in brief, nervous flashes, my brother and I had never been able to truly convey to each other the emotional kinship between us. We had never really been able to express it, enjoy it, sustain each

other through it, make anything of it in our lives. We may have wanted to—and I think, as we grew older, that both of us truly did—but we just couldn't manage it. There had been too much history between us; too many cruel gibes and long silences, too much fear. And that was why whenever we said hello we were already edging away, already saying goodbye.

And when I finally understood all of this, fully and deeply, I was able to forgive both of us for the chances we had missed with each other and would never have again. Given who we were, and given the world in which we found ourselves, Bob and I had done the absolute best we could. And as that recognition deepened within me over the next weeks and months, I felt my grief lifting. A measure of peace and energy returned to me. And unexpectedly, as the pain receded, I began to feel Bob's presence more vividly. While before I had been able to think of my brother only with sadness and longing, I was now beginning to remember him also with amused affection, to be able to enjoy memories of his con-man charm, his absurdist humor, his breathtaking, unstoppable energy.

I did not stop missing my brother then. I still miss him greatly, and I expect that I always will. But sensing Bob's spirit nearby—chortling, manic, ready for the next high-stakes game—helps me fill the space where he once was.[9]

In *No Time for Good Byes,* Janice Harris Lord sums up the idea:

You may find yourself falling into old patterns of behavior in an effort to protect your parents. You may feel that they hurt enough without having to watch you grieve. You may go to incredible lengths to hide your pain from them. It may seem right for you to make decisions for your parents or take on parental responsibilities in an effort to care for them. You may end up "parenting your parents." Usually, though, adult children and parents care for one another because it gives them something to do with their grief. Ask if your parents feel you are over-protecting or mothering them. Respect their response and accommodate them as best you can.

In some ways you may feel as though, in addition to the loss of your sibling, you have lost your parents. Your parents may always have been strong and available for you in times of crisis. Even if you aren't very close to your parents, it can be incredibly painful to become aware of their vulnerability and weakness. This may be the first time you've turned to your parents for support and they can't solve the problem and make it better for you. You may need to grieve the loss of your parents, the parents that were always strong, always in control, never vulnerable.

Like watching a rock tossed into the lake, you may experience other losses connected with your sibling's death. If your brother or sister married, your family may lose contact with the husband or wife, and with the children. If you want to stay close with them, you may have to be direct about your desires and take the responsibility for staying in touch. Eventually most widows and widowers remarry, which can be a source of hurt to the family of the dead husband or wife. Remember, if you can, that no one will replace your brother or sister, and remarrying isn't an act of disloyalty. A new spouse will probably feel very uncertain about his or her relationship with your family, and will welcome some clarification.[10]

The loss of your sibling is a major loss and carries with it a number of complications. From caring for your parents and grandparents to the dynamics involved with other siblings, you will probably re-experience some of your family history and losses that you have not visited in some time. This can be upsetting, but it can also be an opportunity for you to renew and rebuild relationships.

8

The Loss of a Friend

Friends are invaluable. They enrich our lives in ways we don't always comprehend until they're gone. Who you are today is because of your friendships. They have helped shape you. Much of what I have learned is from my friends. In a sense, a friend is a teacher.

When we experience the death of someone, we want our loss to be validated. But it's often lacking when we let others know that a friend has died. The brief responses of some seem like courtesy comments. We want them to at least acknowledge our grief. Perhaps they assume we have lots of friends and one won't be missed.

The impact of a close friend on you is life changing.

In a friendship relationship, you will come to a greater understanding of who you are in Christ and as a person. When you engage in intimate sharing and experience transparency, your facades drop away, and you learn to confront who you really are in a new way. One of the blessings of friendship is personal growth as a follower of Christ.

A friend is someone who senses your struggles and is there to help carry your load: "There is a friend who sticks closer than a brother" (Prov. 18:24). Friends will help answer your questions and solve your problems. They provide a listening ear and assist you in seeing what you may be blind to by yourself. You no longer feel alone in your struggles, and there is comfort in knowing that someone is standing beside you.[1]

The Value of Friendship

Here is how several authors describe the value of friendship:

> Relationships provide healing, both spiritual and psychological. Spiritual healing and maturity is fostered by those who encourage and affirm us and by those who tutor us in the ways of God. Psychological healing is aided by the laughter and the tears that all

good relationships offer. When you feel bruised and beaten, misunderstood and rejected, a true friend is like an oasis in a parched desert. True friendship means that there is someone beside you who cares.[2]

Don't be surprised if you grieve more for a friend than you did for a recently deceased relative. The old saying, "You pick your friends, relatives are thrust upon you," holds true here. Friends are special people in our lives because we choose them to be. Friends fill time in our lives that will be vacant when they die. Besides, friends are usually close to us in age, and when they die we are reminded of our own mortality. Thus their deaths can have an acute impact on us. They give rise to the thought, "It could have been me."

The death of a friend presents its own problems. Friends seldom are involved in the funeral planning or are consulted on the disposition of keepsakes and memories. The grief felt by a friend seldom draws the sympathy or concern given to close relatives. At the same time, family members may expect you to attend to various tasks because you were a friend of the deceased, not realizing how much you yourself are grieving the loss of your friend.[3]

Close friends often provide emotional, physical, spiritual, even financial support during the deceased's life, especially during a prolonged illness. When the friend dies, these helpers are expected to transfer emotional and spiritual (in some instances physical or financial) support to the family. Transferred affection may be limited to the duration of the rituals or a short time thereafter. Some conclude that anything less than full, unquestioned cooperation with the chief mourner betrays the friendship. Some families do take advantage of the generosity and hospitality of friends.[4]

The level of intimacy between close friends is higher than many other social relationships, including those of biological relatedness.

Friendships that have endured also have greater demands than from other interests, and so forth. Because of the uniqueness of the experience of friendship, the death of a friend is a profound loss. Moving through this grief is often complicated because of the lack of sensitivity to the need of friends in grief.[5]

Biblical Stories of Friendship

Remember the biblical story of Jonathan and David?

On several occasions, King Saul attempted to kill David. Torn between his loyalty to his father and his friendship with David, Jonathan initially denied his father's actions. But when David fled into the desert for his life, Jonathan went out to his friend "and helped him find strength in God" (1 Sam. 23:16). How strange a situation: the son of the man trying to kill David was the one who comforted him!

The two friends assumed that their friendship would continue after Saul's death and into David's kingship. But

Jonathan, two of his brothers, and King Saul died in a battle. When David heard of the death of his friend, he wept and refused to eat. Eventually, through great pain, he composed a lament that he ordered be taught to the men of his army:

> Your glory, O Israel, lies slain on your heights.
> How the mighty have fallen!...
> Saul and Jonathan—
> in life they were loved and gracious,
> and in death they were not parted.
> They were swifter than eagles,
> they were stronger than lions...
> How the mighty have fallen in battle!
> Jonathan lies slain on your heights.
> I grieve for you, Jonathan my brother,
> you were very dear to me.
> your love was wonderful,
> More wonderful than that of women.
> How the mighty have fallen! (2 Sam. 1:19,23,25-27).

This lament is a window into the close friendship of these two men and a hint of the potential depth of friendship.[6]

Jesus stood by the grave of a friend. Scripture says that He was "deeply moved in spirit and troubled" (John 11:33). He knew He would raise His friend in minutes, and yet He wept.

A Hole in Our Lives

A deep, significant friendship takes years of involvement. The older we get, the more we expect others to age or die. Our friends fill roles in our life. Some may have mentored us, or we them. When a friend dies, there's an ache, or hole, in our lives. We feel cut off from someone significant in our life. The authors of *I Wasn't Ready to Say Goodbye* describe it this way:

> When a close friend dies suddenly, it is natural to feel cut off from your source of advice and companionship. Thrown into the ever-present reality of the moment, there you are with your questions, your fears, your celebrations, and

your friend isn't there to share them with you. In the past, your friend would have been beside you at a moment like this.[7]

Friendship can often impact belief. For example, writer Philip Yancey's belief in Easter and resurrection was shaped by the death of three close friends in separate accidents within a one-year period:

> One reason I am open to belief, I admit, is that at a very deep level I want the Easter story to be true. Faith grows out of the subsoil of yearning, and something instinctive in human beings cries out against the reign of Death. Whether hope takes the form of Egyptian pharaohs stashing their jewels and chariots in pyramids, or the modern American obsession with keeping bodies alive until the last possible nanosecond and then preserving them with embalming fluid in double-sealed caskets, we humans resist the ideas of death having the final say. We want to believe otherwise.

I remember the year I lost three close friends in separate accidents. Above all else, I want for Easter to be true because of its promise that one day I will get my friends back.

I believe in the resurrection primarily because I have gotten to know God. I know that God is love, and I also know that we human beings want to keep alive those whom we love. I do not let my friends die, they live on in my memory and my heart long after I have stopped seeing them ... God will not let death win.[8]

The Gratitude of Friendship

Henry David Thoreau said, "Even the death of friends will inspire us as much as their lives.... Their memories will be entrusted over the sublime and pleasing thoughts, as monuments of other men are overgrown with moss; for our friends have no place in the graveyard."[9] The Roman philosopher Seneca said, "To lose a friend is the greatest of all evils, but endeavor rather to rejoice that you possessed him than to mourn his loss."[10]

How do we handle the years we've spent with a friend? With gratitude. It's as simple as that. As Robert Buckman states in *I Didn't Know What to Say:*

> I have reconciled the deaths of friends by being grateful for having had such friendships. I have come to understand that Death ends life but certainly doesn't rob it of meaning. We all need to remember that in our lives we affect and change the people closest to us. Those changes have a considerable value. For instance, I am not the same person that I would have been had I not met James, Ruth, John or the many others who have made a lasting impression on me. Some people even think of these changes as some form of immortality. They suggest that people who have died, or who are dying, do live on, in changes they have caused in those who survive them. Having a library or office block named after you cannot make people remember you. But if you've

altered the way people think, then some of the meaning of your life will go on after your death.[11]

John Carmody notes the following in *Toward a Male Spirituality:*

I am not interested in "embalming" the memory of my friends, and embalming was quite sufficient. Rather, I want the vibrant memories of the friendships to be the raw materials for future growth and the new friendships—not to replace friends gone but instead to complement those friendships, which are only "on hold" at the moment. Quite candidly, I am still working on the verbs. I have not gotten used to saying, "I had a friend named Rusty" because I believe I still have a friend named Rusty and that I will see him again.

Knowing the living God means knowing why it is reasonable to hope that one will survive the grave. Concomitantly, it is finding a reason to hope that all the precious relationships we developed on earth will be preserved in heaven.[12]

Harold Ivan Smith sums it up as follows:

Some things cannot easily be explained,
they belong to a realm called faith.
How can I speak of an unending or
never-ending friendship
when I've just come from my friend's
fresh grave?
Although all my intellect tells me that
such thinking, such a hope is fantasy,
of a variety best jettisoned in childhood.
Well, I have chosen to believe
that my friendship still exists,
that my friendship waits to be resumed.
I have chosen to believe my friends are with me
not merely in a memory slice
but in a realm
for which the English language

has not yet created adequate vocabulary.[13]

You may know more about your friend than some of his or her family knows. Reminisce with the family; you could be a conveyor of stories they would like to hear.

The Investment of Friendship

Over the years, I served on a Family Board for Pepperdine University. One of the other members was radio and television host Art Linkletter, and it was a special privilege to meet him and then have several conversations with him. One day, we were talking and he said, "I'm 94, and all of my friends have died. I don't have the years left to build new friendships." So true.

It takes years of investment to build a significant connection with someone. I have several very close friendships. All of these people are older than 60, and some are in their mid-seventies. With one of these friends, we have talked about giving a eulogy at one another's memorial. This means we have to film it prior since one wouldn't be able to speak (obviously)! We have been friends for more than 40 years. We have ministered together, hunted and fished together, prayed and wept together. We both lost sons by the name of Matthew while they were in their early twenties, and we lost our wives within three months of each other to cancer.

I hear about friends who have died. I read about it in magazines or alumni papers or over the phone. And I wonder, *Who will be next? He was younger than I am. Why him and not me?* And then I begin to remember. It's as if a highway of memories begins to unfold.

The older you get, the more your network of friendship begins to diminish. One of the phrases you may hear from others is, "It was just a friend." Books on loss and grief give no attention to friends as grievers. You are left out, ignored, unrecognized. Isn't it interesting, though, that even though most people don't acknowledge a friend's death, a common phrase is,

"What's wrong, you look like you've lost your best friend"?

Have you ever read an obituary that listed no immediate survivors? This is referring to relatives, but it excludes friends, which can be offensive to them. Unfortunately, grieving has become a family affair in our culture. Even the closest of friends won't be recognized or have legitimate mourning opportunity. Not only that, but you're likely to be ignored by the immediate family or brought in to help with the funeral arrangements and required to negate your own grief to help with the needs of the family.

Friends usually notify other friends and, unfortunately, there are too many notifications on Facebook.

"I want to say a few things about my friend..." is often heard. We may be asked, or we may choose to give, a eulogy. Giving one is emotionally draining and demanding. Often the eulogy of a friend can have a greater impact than a family member's. Friends share more personal and unknown insights.

What if you didn't have the opportunity to give a eulogy at the service? You can write out your own eulogy and read it to others or read it at the gravesite. You could mail it to family members of the deceased.

Honoring Your Friend

It is important to remember your friend. The only person I know who has written at length on grieving a friend is a friend of mine named Harold Ivan Smith, and in the following section I have borrowed extensively from his work. Harold wrote the following:

> Healthy remembering has two goals: "to review and remember realistically" and to "revive and re-experience the old feelings."
>
> It is easier to dance with the memories than to invest energy trying not to remember. Many friends find making a collage to be a wonderful way to sort through memory bytes to construct a cherishable memory of this friend. Healthy grief relies on revisiting places of importance, viewing photo

albums or videos, or telling stories. I remind grievers that a friend is not gone until two things happen (both of which require decisions on the part of the friend-griever): (1) friends stop saying the name and (2) friends stop telling stories about the deceased. Something wonderful can happen when someone says, "Do you remember the time _____...?"

In the Christian scriptures read during the Eucharist, there is a strong admonition to remember. Jesus, instituting the Eucharist on the eve of his death, prodded friends, "And as often as you do this, remember me" (paraphrase of 1 Corinthians 11:25). The Greek tense is imperative: *remember me!* Jesus, facing death, had reason to fear that his friends might, in time, forget him; after all, one friend had already betrayed him. Thus, those who practice the Christian faith, have a strong precedent for remembering.[14]

One way you can honor your friend is by attending the rituals for that friend, which include the visitation, calling hours or wake; the funeral or memorial service; the committal or scattering.

The visitation is an historic ritual that has come to be valued more by some friends than the funeral. A secondary benefit of the visitation is that by having the gathering for the primary friends at a funeral home, the privacy of the family is preserved for the primary mourners.

Some friends—particularly those who think attendance is an obligation—prefer to attend the visitation or wake rather than the funeral, specifically because there is little time for social interaction or conversation.[15]

You may be asked to just "be there" or provide support by:
- Calling the family on the phone or going to the primary residence upon learning of the death
- Sending flowers (unless the family has made a "no flowers" decision)
- Donating to a designated charity in honor of the friend who has died
- Attending various rituals, especially the visitation/wake and, if possible,

the memorial service/funeral and the burial/scattering
- Preparing or donating food for the residence or preparing a meal for the family
- Volunteering to provide assistance—"If there is anything I can do, please call me"
- Fulfilling specific family requests: "Could you go to the airport and pick up his brother?" or "Would you answer the phone for us?"
- Supplying missing data: "Who was her accountant? Where did she bank?"

Did you experience any of these in the death of your friend? If specifically invited by the chief mourner, you may have offered support by:
- Offering advice on decisions: "What do you think we should do about...?" or "You knew her. What do you think she would want for music at the funeral?"
- Having a part (as defined by the family) in the funeral/memorial service or committal
- Delivering a eulogy

- Serving as an active or honorary casket/pall/urn bearer

In recent years, the friend has come to be a passive, secondary participant unless the family specifically invites or assigns more active participation. The friend may volunteer to run errands, help with arrangements or host out-of-town relatives. Friends do not, however, volunteer to deliver the eulogy or be a pallbearer. Volunteering for either honor may be perceived to be an infringement upon the family's freedom to choose. Some families would find such an offer intrusive. On the other hand, some families might feel obligated, especially when the friend has been helpful during a long illness, "After all he has done, how can we refuse?"[16]

Ways to Remember Your Friend

The following are several practical ways to remember your friend:
- *Say* your friend's name aloud when telling a story or talking about her.

- *Attend* the rituals honoring your friend.
- *Adopt* one of your friend's charities. Loss of donors through death hurts great causes, institutions and organizations. A donation—even if small—on the birth date or death date or Memorial Day or a religious holiday is a meaningful way to remember a friend.
- *Write* a note to the family with a specific anecdote about your friend. If you send a card, add a handwritten note with an "I will always remember the time, _____..." or "one thing that made _____ such a special friend was..."
- *Check in* by phone or letter with some of your friend's friends.
- *Go ahead* and say what you were thinking: "_____, my friend, would have loved this," even if only to yourself.
- *Have* a calligrapher take a favorite quotation of a friend and create a memory-in-ink.
- *Write* a letter to the editor of the newspaper telling the city what a great friend you've lost.

- *Place* a memoriam notice on the anniversary of the death or on your friend's birthday.
- *Remember:* Your grief counts! So do what you need to do to grieve healthily.[17]

Harold Ivan Smith, in his unique way, captures the impact of the loss of a friend as follows:

> "Oh, but you have lots of
> friends..."
> Left is the word they do not say.
> That's what people told me when
> I mentioned
> my friend's death.
> Although I am blessed
> with a rich bounty of friends
> I am still diminished
> by the loss of any one of them.
> Because with each friend's passing
> a chunk of my past and future
> ends.
> Who will be there to ask,
> "Do you remember the time?"
>
> No one, these days,
> has friends to spare.
> It would be like saying
> to the curator of an art museum

after a masterpiece had been stolen,
"Oh, but you still have lots of paintings…"
Perhaps.
"But I had only one that hung there."

Give your grief its voice.
Pay attention to your memories.
And count the ways you have been enriched
by having such a friend.[18]

It may help to read this aloud to your friends. As I wrote this chapter I decided to write to my group of significant friends and share this piece of writing with them. I don't want to miss out.

9

The Loss of a Pet

When your pet dies, you've probably lost a friend and a family member. Those of us who love our animals know this is true. An animal lover's life has been enhanced in a healthy way, and yes, there will be those who don't understand, and that's all right.

Our pets are special, and when they die or are lost, we ache because of the hole in our heart. Some don't like the terminology of "pet," but prefer "companion."

Pets have become a major part of the lives of so many people. They fulfill a number of needs for many of us. They fulfill a need to nurture and care for something or someone. It's a sharing of our life with another living being that is not a human. Our pets provide love and acceptance; and for many, this relationship may be better than with some of our family members. One writer described what we experience:

It has often been noted that pets can be truer friends than others of our own species. They are never critical, and therefore allow us to blossom emotionally in ways that would not be possible with fellow humans, who tend to be competitive and judgmental. We make our companion animals our secret sharers, often with greater intimacy and trust than that which is often given to the people who are closest to us. Our bonds with beloved pets are in many ways stronger, purer, and far more intimate than with others of our own species. We feel loved and completely secure in sharing our secret souls with them.

Some pets are so innocent and transparent in their needs and feelings that we get to know and trust them better than most humans. And they feel the same about us.[1]

Sometimes the death of a pet not only leaves us in grief, but we also lose the buffer we had against other stresses in our life, and now we're forced to face them. Perhaps we used our pet to cover other losses in our life. If so, this is an opportunity to face those losses and resolve them.

Many are surprised by the depth and extent of their emotional response to the death of their pet. If your pet has died, you won't be able to cope with the emotions and process them until you admit them and release the intensity. Yes, it hurts to admit or acknowledge them, but this is the way to learn to control them. Writing or drawing is a healthy way to drain the intensity of the loss.

Social Losses

One of the losses we experience with the loss of a pet is the loss of touch. We often touch our pets more than the people in our life. Our pets reach out to touch us, and we do the same. There's a benefit to this, for we are comforted and calmed by this interaction. So when your pet died, there was a void, since this was a major part of your life.

You also lost part of your daily routine and now have to adjust. Who did you see and/or talk to first thing in the morning? The morning affection, touch, feeding, letting your pet out, fetching the paper, grooming are gone; so too the routine of the day and evening have disappeared. Your pet may have been the greeter as well as your built-in protection and watchdog. Can you think of other changes or losses you're experiencing?

Did you ever make up stories in your head about what went on in your pet's head? Did you ever wonder what your pet was thinking? Most of us do. Sometimes we wonder what our pets are thinking as well as how they feel about us. And yes, we do make up stories about what goes on in their minds. We all need an attachment to others, to someone who provides a sense of security and protection and comfort you can count on. Our animals don't change as people do—they can be a constant in our life.

Although our animals' ability to speak is limited, we fine-tune our sensibilities to such an extent that we feel certain we know almost everything about them. We know their needs. We know what they're feeling. We feel good about figuring out what they want or what they're doing and why.

Most of us carry on conversations with our pets. If you have a dog, you probably greet your dog when you arrive home and say goodbye when you leave. You ask questions like, "Are you hungry?" or "Do you want to go for a walk?" You even ask them questions they couldn't possibly answer: "Should I wear this suit, or go casual?" or "Do you think it's going to stay warm, or should I take a coat today?"

For most of us, our language changes under different circumstances. We talk differently in formal situations than with family and friends. There's a special kind of language we use when talking with dogs. We call this form of language *doggerel.* It's true! It's different. Do you know how it's different? Think about this: With adults we usually use 10 to 11 words per sentence; but with dogs, we use about 4.

When you talk to your dog, about 90 percent of your conversation will be about the present; after all, why bring up the past with your dog, or anyone else for that matter. And you're 20 times more likely to repeat or rephrase statements than when talking to a person.

Most of what we say to dogs is of a social nature rather than items of information.

We also use higher tones and distort words and phrases to make them sound less formal. We place more emphasis on tone of voice. And finally, we (yes, we as people) tend to mimic the sounds our dogs make!

We all have memories of a pet. But just like the memories of a loved one we lost in death, in time these memories fade, and this is another loss. Capturing memories of your pet at this time will help you later on. Here are some questions that may help you identify them:
- When and where did you obtain your pet?
- What did you think and feel when you first saw your companion?

- Why did you choose your pet's name?
- What were your pet's physical features?
- What was your pet's personality like?
- What did your pet learn from you?
- What was your pet able to do?
- What special memories do you have?
- What are you missing the most at this time?

Let's consider your grief over the loss of your pet. First of all, we live in a culture that doesn't talk about loss, death and grief, and doesn't want to. There isn't an abundance of encouragement to talk about loss and grief over a person let alone a pet. We don't have an understanding environment in which to grieve. Half of our population doesn't own a dog or cat, so they will not understand your grief. Because of this, you may have to be careful where you grieve for your pet.

One of the best ways to help yourself as well as others is to write a letter or card that gives clear information about your loss. Describe your pet, how long you were together, what your pet meant to you, and so on. Tell about your grief and the fact that this will continue for some time. Share what kind of response would be helpful and ask for patience and understanding, especially if others don't have pets and may not understand your loss. Others will appreciate a card and letter such as this since it's like a road map to follow. Most individuals don't know what to say and how to respond. They don't know what to say when a person dies let alone a pet. In chapter 1, "The World of Grief," there are some guidelines you can use to share with others what you are going through.

You need people you can trust and who will understand. Some will be supportive. Some may even think something is wrong with you because of your grief. Many have found support through organizations and groups of individuals on the Internet.

Issues that Affect the Way You Mourn

Mourning the death of your pet is different from mourning the death of a person. You won't receive the recognition or support over this loss like you do when it is a person. There are few rituals for mourning this loss.

Remember that we all grieve differently. Even in your family you may have had a deep attachment to your pet while for others the relationship with the pet was casual or even typified by a sense of toleration. The stronger your attachment, the deeper your grief. If you had mixed feelings about your pet when he or she was alive (always chewing some part of the furniture or going potty on your favorite flowers), you may have mixed feelings after he or she dies.

The way in which your pet died could also affect your grief. If your pet's death was unexpected or sudden, you can expect to feel shock and numbness that will prolong your loss. If it was a progressive or lingering painful illness, this will impact you as well.

Who you are as a person affects your grief. Your personality is reflected even in your grief. Some people like to talk with others about it, while others just want to talk to themselves. The amount of support you have from others will also impact your grief. It's more difficult to grieve in isolation than with the loving support of others. It's important to find others who understand, care and are nonjudgmental.

If there are additional unresolved losses in your life at this time, or major changes, this will also affect your grieving. The more losses or stresses in your life, the more difficult or prolonged your grief may be.[2]

When a Pet Is Euthanized

If you had to have your pet euthanized, it's a difficult decision that is not made lightly by most. Many pet owners struggle with that decision, and even when they know it was the best one, they question it and wish there had been another choice, which there wasn't.

We commonly use the word "euthanize," but most peoople don't know that it is a Greek word that means "happy or fortunate in death."

For many animals, euthanasia was best to avoid prolonging their suffering.

The most likely emotion to experience if you have euthanized your pet is guilt. The most prevailing thought is that you killed your pet. You had to make a decision you didn't want to make and wish someone else had made for you.

But the other emotion is relief. It's normal to feel this when your pet no longer suffers and his or her pain is gone. There is also personal relief since you no longer have to clean up after your pet or medicate it or carry it around. Sometimes the feeling of relief intensifies your sense of guilt and you go through a mental battle, feeling awful that you feel relief that your pet is dead. You may struggle with the thought, *Would I do it again?* if you could have your pet back. But this is forgetting why this act was necessary in the first place. Your guilt is an indication of the intensity of love you had for your pet.

Both guilt and relief are normal. Most people struggle with these. No one needs to feel condemnation for either.

Can you say, "I am normal for feeling both guilt and relief, and this is all right"? It's difficult to reason with any of our emotions, especially these two, which seem to contradict each another.

There are no benefits to guilt if you did something in error or made a mistake or were misinformed; guilt is only helpful to guide you to correct whatever occurred so that it doesn't happen in the future. As Moira Anderson Allen states in *Coping with Sorrow on the Loss of Your Pet:*

> The feelings you have toward your pet are genuine and deep. You need not to be embarrassed about them or feel childish or ashamed. As with any grief, it is important to acknowledge the loss and its meaning to you personally. It is important to allow yourself to cry, to drag out pictures, to talk with a sympathetic person about how special this pet was to you. In this way you can work through the initial stages of grief. Let yourself feel the loss and the absence of the loved one.[3]

Putting Your Loss in Perspective

There is something worse than having a pet you grieve over. It's having one that you didn't grieve over!

When most of us lose a pet, we would prefer for it to die naturally and painlessly. This frees us up from having to make the difficult decision to euthanize it to save it from suffering. But remember that your animal was an animal. People and animals differ in many ways. You and I can make moral choices. We have a conscience, so we can think about what is right and what is wrong. You and I know we'll die. We are aware of pain and loss. We know that sickness is a part of our life. We know that God exists and loves us. We have a sense of time.

Animals do none of the above. Your pet was a creature who lived by instinct—yes, emotions and pain are a part of a pet's life, but they don't think about them or dwell on them. They die; but unlike us, they don't spend time thinking about it. They sense our emotions and can read them, but not our minds. Perhaps you had to euthanize your pet. You may have mixed feelings about it, like most of us would. There was a reason you chose to do this. It may be helpful for you to make a list of these reasons to help you accept your decision. Your pet was not put on this earth to suffer or barely live its life. Your pet didn't want to be impaired and not function like he or she was supposed to—running, eating, eliminating outside and being pain free.[4]

Guilt—the emotion—is a gigantic waste of time. Guilt usually comes from having done something wrong. You didn't. Could you convince a jury in a courtroom that you did something wrong with your pet? Does guilt serve any purpose? Not for you, nor for your pet.

Fortunately for your pet, guilt is unknown. You and I are the ones who have to fight its presence. It doesn't infect the life of our pets. I've never met a dog or cat that feels guilty over eating part of the bed. I've never seen my golden retrievers beat up on themselves for making a mistake.

You may experience guilt for doing or not doing something with your pet. Perhaps it was not giving them enough medical care or time. Perhaps it was deciding to euthanize. Jan Katz, who has written extensively about animals, has this to say about guilt:

When it comes to making decisions about animals in distress or at the end of their lives, guilt seems to be the silent partner, the unacknowledged elephant in the room. It is a powerful force, one I hope you will manage to avoid.

Guilt is tied to the decisions we make. In fact, the more decisions we make about the death of our dogs and cats, the more likely we are to feel guilty about them. Should we have tried more medication? Another surgery? Spent more money? Tried another vet? Waited?

These decisions are tough. Despite all of the books and websites and blogs, when it comes to making choices about the deaths of our animals, we are on our own. We never will know for sure if the decisions we make are the right ones. That's the lonely truth of it. There's no one—no force, no expert, or guru—who can tell us that we did the right thing. We must convince ourselves of that.[5]

In *Saying Good-bye to the Pet You Love,* Lorri A. Greene and Jacquelyn Landis note:

> In its simplest definition, guilt is a thought triggered by a past event. It is a very normal response to the perception that, somehow, we have failed our companion animals. No matter what the circumstances of their pet's death, most people feel some degree of guilt if they have chosen to euthanize their companion animal, even more so if they have killed it accidentally. Very few people ever feel it's the right time to lose their pet. Unfortunately, our companion animals do not usually live as long as we do.[6]

One of my close friends shared with me his experience with his dog, Buck:

> Hi Norm,

As you know it's been a hard day today, with a lot of tears in getting Buck's grave dug and then taking him to the vet at 3:00PM. It was his liver that failed and probably was cancerous, that's what took him so fast. The vet gave me an option of trying to reverse some of the issues if it wasn't cancer but she told me that the chances of it working in a dog his age and this weak was slim, but she wanted to at least give me the option. He was starting to have a lot of pain and his hind legs were so weak that he could hardly get up when he was lying down. I knew it was time.

It's late and dark, so I'm not sure if I'm going to bury him tonight or in the morning. One thing for sure is that I'm really going to miss him and his always being at the gate, waiting for me to come home ... he was so devoted to me and trying to please me unconditionally right up to the end. I felt terrible while digging his grave since he came out and laid down by where I was digging and just watched me dig ... but that's just Buck. He always wanted to be as close to me as he could get.

Well, thanks for your prayers. I really needed them today. I was just so thankful we have had these two extra days to be with him and say goodbye ... and hold him as he went.

Dale

Gaining Closure After Losing a Pet

What are some additional steps to take that could help? Some have found it beneficial to rearrange your surroundings. With the loss of your pet you may be bombarded with reminders—toys, bed, special places inside and outside the house. It helps to do some rearrangement if at all possible. Change what you can so you're not always looking for your pet where it always stayed. You may want to put your pet's possessions out of sight for a while, but don't give them away. Many have found that in time they provide a connection with fond memories. Some want to save them for their next pet, while others prefer not to.

Changing your schedule on purpose may help. If you fed your pet at a certain time or went for a walk at a particular time, when these times roll around, your feeling of "without" hits you. If you have difficulty with these times, one solution is to change your schedule and bring something new into these times. Make a list of other possible activities you could engage in to fill those times and then try some of them. If you walked a certain route, choose a new route. Make a list of your best memories with your pet and read them out loud. Some write about it in a journal. Others have written a thank-you letter to their pet. I took out a full-page memorial in the *Golden Retriever Journal* as an expression of my feelings for my first golden retriever, Sheffield. I've also written stories about him in my dog books. I delight now in reading those stories.

If you have other pets, don't neglect them. They need your care and attention. You still have a companion.

Cats have grieved over the loss of a cat or dog, and dogs have grieved over the loss of other animals as well. Yes, the others could be a painful reminder of the one you've lost, but caring for them and giving them love can help you.

Pets notice changes of any kind, even new furniture or arrangements, or new routine. They also notice who is missing. Many observe grief reactions in remaining pets. I have always had two dogs. At first I had Shelties, and for the last 20 years, golden retrievers. When one dies, I see changes in the remaining dog. Some animals mope when there is a loss. Your other pets can react like other family members. Even if the animals didn't get along that well, there is still a bond there and they can miss one another.

To help reach a sense of closure, here are some suggestions:

- *Make a list* —Itemize particular times and situations that still give you special pain and trouble in your bereavement. Continue expanding this over several days. Later, read it over and look for a common denominator.

Any repeated themes? To help put this into better perspective, it is best to discuss your list and themes with someone you trust and respect.

• *Don't berate yourself for not feeling as much pain as you first did*—Sometimes we tend to get anxious about what may feel like a too rapid or even a too slow recovery. The healing process makes us stronger and better, but it involves pain, time and self-respect. And it takes lots of patience.[7]

If there are other members in your family, gather them together and ask each one to share what they remember about your pet or a favorite story or experience. You may learn some things you didn't know or you may discover feelings you didn't know existed on their part. If you have guilt, perhaps they share in your feelings of guilt and blame as well. A therapist suggested:

By bringing these different issues of guilt and blame into the open, you and your family may be able to realize that there was no single cause of death to blame, no single person responsible, and that these individual feelings have no basis in reality but are simply getting in the way of the healing process.[8]

I've had counselees tell me the story of their pet, not just once but several times. You may want to tell the story to a trusted friend who is a good listener. Tell it from the birth of your pet to his or her death and leave nothing out. Put in as many details as possible, from the good times to the bad times, the funny times to the painful times. For some it has helped them realize that feelings they have struggled with such as anger, blame or guilt have no basis in reality, and it gives them a different perspective of what happened at the end of their pet's life.

Helping Children Adjust to a Pet's Death

If you have children or grandchildren, the death of your pet can have a major impact upon them. If your pet was older, it could be that your children can't remember life without the cat or dog. Sometimes a pet is closer to a child than to other family members. I was an only child for the most part, and my cat and Collie were like my siblings. I could tell them everything. Every day after school, for several years, when I got home from school, I took my Collie and my BB gun and we roamed the hills of Hollywood.

For a child, a pet is security. A pet doesn't tease you but is there for you. One therapist said:

> Pets were our allies against the world, friends who were always on our side when parents picked on us, siblings harassed us, human friends abandoned us and bullies made our lives miserable. Those of us who remember times like these know how devastating the loss of a pet can be to our own children.[9]

Let your children, whether younger or older, share their feelings and reactions to your pet's death, and encourage them to ask their questions. Hopefully you have been honest with your child about your pet's illness and death (if your child is younger, read chapter 4 in this book on children and death). As a parent or grandparent, our task is to help and allow our children to grieve. If your children don't say anything to you, remember that they are talking to themselves about it. Encourage them to talk or draw their thoughts or feelings, and just listen. And remember that neither you nor they need to be fixed, since neither of you is broken.

If your child heard the phrase "Your pet was *put to sleep,*" you will need to clarify what this means and provide better terminology for what happened.

Sometimes we or others make comments to our children that we need to clarify such as, "God loved him, so He took him back to heaven," or "The dog doctor made a mistake and your dog died," or "It was just a hamster," or "Our cat went to sleep forever." The phrase, "Our pet was put to sleep" can create fear about going to sleep or having any surgical procedure.

Here are numerous suggestions on helping your child adjust to a pet's death, which come from Dr. Wallace

Sife, a leading specialist on pet bereavement:

1. Encourage your child to ask all the questions they can think of about death and dying. When you don't know the answer, admit it and let them know you'll find the answer for them.
2. You could hold a ceremony for your pet that includes your child. Any type of structured ritual can be helpful, especially if it involves the entire family and the child sees that other family members grieve as well.
3. It helps if all of you reminisce about your pet and share favorite stories and experiences. These could be written or drawn and then shared.
4. Check with the librarian at school or your city to find books that include the death of a pet as part of the story.
5. At an appropriate time discuss together the possibility of another pet in the future. When you do get another pet, suggest that your child tells your new pet stories about the

pet that died and suggest that both pets could have been good friends.
6. Visit animal farms and animal shelters to learn more about animals you're not going to adopt and get to learn more about them.
7. Let others in your child's life know about the loss.
8. If euthanasia was used, talk about this with your child as well as the reasons.[10]

Here are some suggestions of things to say to your child:
- Your pet was important to you. Let's talk about your relationship with your pet (always use the name of the animal).
- Most children talk to their animals—what about you?
- What did you talk about?
- Did you talk about secrets or problems?
- Where did your pet sleep?
- Did you celebrate your pet's birthday?
- Was your pet your best friend? If so, why?
- Do you have a drawing, or could you make one?

- Like most of us, you probably miss _____. What do you do to get rid of your hurt?
- Someday, would you like another pet?

Some of the suggestions for recovering from the loss of your pet would be similar to the loss of a person:

- Find caring and supportive people to share your grief.
- Write a letter or a will from your pet to yourself. Some have found it helpful to continue to update it from time to time.
- You may want to dedicate something in memory of your pet. A donation or a plaque or even books have been used.
- It may help to make a memory book and then write a letter to your pet thanking him or her for these memories. Some have done the same with audio recordings.
- Vary your routines at home. Change some of your patterns in terms of times and places that involved your pet (this was mentioned earlier in the chapter).

- Visit with other pet owners and their pets. Share your stories together.
- Gradually put away personal possessions of your pet and store them out of sight until you're ready to get rid of them.
- List your thoughts and feelings each month and you'll discover how you are moving forward in your grief. There are pet grief groups available.
- Visit the animal shelter or animal training classes just to interact.[11]
- Tell yourself your grief is normal and it's all right to take as long as you need to grieve.
- Remember that your sense of relief is a positive response. Things are now better for both you and your pet, even though because of your emotions you question it. Guilt is a negative response that is detrimental to how you see yourself as well as your feelings of relief. It needs to be challenged so that it doesn't gain a foothold in your mind. Guilt can distort reality as well as specific facts.[12]

When a Pet Is Lost

Death isn't the only way we lose a pet. Pets disappear. They run away or are stolen or get away when you're at the mall. And when they disappear, they may be gone forever. But you don't know the outcome, and some say this is worse than a death. We call this an ambiguous loss. There is no closure. You are denied seeing your pet's body or having a service; and you didn't have the opportunity to prepare for its death. This almost happened to Martha.

I helped at the devastating aftermath of Hurricane Katrina. It was a story of loss—the loss of homes, cars, a culture, people and pets. So many pets were lost with very few recovered. Such was the case of Martha, who had lived in a small older house in the Ninth Ward of New Orleans with her small dog, Fritz. One night the waters of the hurricane swept through aided by multiple breaks in the levee, and the floodwaters rose faster than anyone could imagine. Rescue workers came into Martha's house and moved her to a boat and safety. But in the panic Fritz was forgotten and left behind. It was a few hours later that it dawned on Martha that Fritz had not been rescued, as was the case with thousands of animals in that area. Not only did Martha lose her home and belongings, but also her only remaining family member, Fritz. She was devastated.

Six weeks later, Martha stopped by our Victim Chaplain headquarters at the edge of the Ninth Ward. She wondered if someone could accompany her back to what was left of her home to find Fritz's remains and bury him. The director of Victim Chaplain's said he would be happy to take her. They arrived, went up to the front door, opened it and walked in. Then they heard the sound—a weak "woof" coming from the bathroom.

Looking at one another in shock, they opened the door of the bathroom and there stood Fritz, skin and bones on legs barely able to hold him up. He had existed on water and chewing up anything edible in the confines of that room. He was just hours away from death, so they rushed him to a vet and IVs were started immediately. Today

Martha doesn't have her old home, but she does have something more important—Fritz. Martha was fortunate. What was lost was found. But for most, this isn't the story.

When a pet is lost, you don't know if your pet is dead or alive or healthy or sick or hungry. You end up living with uncertainty as well as guilt, blame, anger and feeling immobilized. You will probably vacillate between grief and hope. You don't know when to begin grieving, and it's often interrupted by the hope that your pet may return. You blame yourself for its loss or you blame another family member. Your routine is disrupted since this loss hangs over your head constantly. You're probably not able to say goodbye, which hinders you from moving on. You're not able to put away the toys or food or get a new pet, but you still need to grieve. Your grief is ongoing.

If your pet has been gone for several weeks, it's probably best to grieve as though it were dead. One of the reasons pet owners have memorial services is that the separation ritual can help you find some sort of closure and move forward.

Celebrating the Life of the Pet and Moving On

One of the positive steps we can take in our recovery from this loss is to celebrate the life of our pet. Remember the best things and experiences about its life. It might help you to consider the following questions:
- Did I give my pet the best life I could?
- Did I feed him every single day of his life?
- Did I care for him when he was sick?
- Did I take him with me whenever I could?
- Did I appreciate and return his affection?
- Did I recognize and honor his true nature?
- Did I love him?
- Do I miss him?
- Did he have a good life?[13]

What about getting another pet? For many, the answer is yes—when you're ready. If so, your new pet is not a replacement. Be sure to take your time and consider your reason for wanting another pet. Will its presence bring you joy and fulfillment, or will it bring sadness and grief? What are your expectations for your new companion? Visit breeders and pet stores. Spend time with other animals before you make a decision. It's important for you and your new pet that you have moved through your grief before you make your choice.

Consider these thoughts as you grieve over your pet:

> Through their deaths, I am opened to the love and light of the world a final gift of feelings, a rebirth of understanding and meaning. Death is as much a part of life as birth. In my grief over them, I see my other losses and sorrows. My sad and fearful childhood, my unhappy mother, my remote and disconnected father, the dreams I have lost and those I have found.
>
> And I see my joy. The friends, the love, the challenges, the change. Is there a better way to

learn and grow? From the darkness, light. From loss, gain. From sorrow, joy. To the animals I have loved and lost, I am nothing but grateful.

> Pain defines love, gives it meaning. Without pain, love is nothing. Grieving hurts, but it cleanses and purifies us and brushes against our souls. It whispers to us that we received the great gift of unconditional love, and *that* does not ever die.[14]

In the future (or now), you may struggle with the thought of obtaining a new pet. You may not want to experience another round of grief. I think what one pet owner said has some merit:

> I hurt so much for people who feel they cannot allow themselves to have another animal once that special pet is gone. By sparing themselves the pain caused by losing a well-loved friend, they are cutting themselves off from so much. Getting a new pet really helps—just think of putting all those bits and pieces you learned from your old friend to use in training

and getting to know a new one. It's not a replacement, it's an enhancement of the affection you felt for your previous pet.[15]

When is the right time? That will be up to you. It's important that you are ready to love a new animal.

A Prayer for Animals

Hear our humble prayer, O God,
for our friends the animals,
especially for animals who are suffering;
for any that are hunted or lost or deserted or
frightened or hungry,
for all that must be put to death.

We entreat for them all thy mercy and pity,
and for those who deal with them we ask
a heart of compassion
and gentle hands and kindly words.

Make us, ourselves, to be true friends to animals,
and so to share the blessings of the merciful.

(Albert Schweitzer)

Recommended Resources

Books

Wallace Sife, Ph.D., *The Loss of a Pet* (New York: Howell Book House, 2005).

Moira Anderson Allen, M.Ed., *Coping with Sorrow on the Loss of Your Pet* (Loveland, CO: Alpine, 1996).

Alan D. Wolfelt, Ph.D., *When Your Pet Dies: A Guide to Mourning, Remembering and Healing* (Fort Collins, CO: Companion Press, 2004).

Organizations

Animal Love and Loss Network (www.alln.org)

The Center for Loss and Life Transition (www.centerforloss.com)

In Memory of Pets: Beyond Life's Gateway (www.in-memory-of-pets.com)

Pet Loss (www.petloss.com). This site maintains an excellent listing of pet loss support groups, counselors and pet cemeteries as well as pet loss hotlines and other websites with helpful pet loss information.

10

The Questions of Life

This is a chapter that may either answer your questions or raise some. You may be ready to read this now, or you may prefer to wait for a while.

There are three questions most often asked by those in grief:
1. Why, God, why?
2. When, God, when?
3. Will I survive, God?

Of those three, why is the most common question of all: Why me? Why now? Why this? Why, God, why? You're not the first person in grief to ask why, and you won't be the last.

You've heard of Job, the man who lost it all in just one day. The book of Job records one devastating loss after another. Job lost his family, his possessions, his wealth and his health. After several days of silence, he began asking the questions many of us ask:

"Why didn't I die at birth?"
"Why can't I die now?"
"Why has God done this to me?"

He threw the question why at God 16 times. Each time there was silence. And you know, silence was probably the best answer. I know that sounds strange; but if God had given Job the answer to his question right away, would Job have accepted it? Would you? Or would you argue and rail against His answer? You probably wouldn't understand God's reason at the time. By not having the answer, we have the opportunity to learn to live by faith.

The prophet Habakkuk asked a few questions in his day as well. Habakkuk was appalled by the suffering he saw around him. Here is his complaint:

> How long, O LORD, must I call for help,
> but you do not listen?
> Or cry out to you, "Violence!"
> but you do not save?
> Why do you make me look at injustice?
> Why do you tolerate wrong?
> Destruction and violence are before me;
> there is strife, and conflict abounds.
> Therefore the law is paralyzed,

and justice never prevails.
The wicked hem in the righteous,
so that justice is perverted (Hab. 1:2-4).

Although Habakkuk's why seemed to go unanswered, he eventually came to the place of confidence and hope. The word "eventually" is important. This acceptance takes time:

Though the fig tree should not blossom,
And there be no fruit on the vines,
Though the yield of the olive should fail,
And the fields produce no food,
Though the flock should be cut off from the fold
And there be no cattle in the stalls,
Yet I will exult in the Lord,
I will rejoice in the God of my salvation
(Hab. 3:17-18, *NASB*).

In spite of everything falling apart, Habakkuk could rejoice in the Lord.

Facing the Furnace

Eventually, you can come to the place of confidence and hope in your time of grief. As you ask God why, also ask Him to help you come to the place where you can say, "In spite of..., I will rejoice."

God does not explain all suffering in the world or the meaning of each loss that occurs. There is no clear explanation for some of the events that take place. God may not answer our why, but He does tell us in whom to trust so that we can endure in the time of trouble. Our why questions are normal, and they're more than questions; often they are protests.

A person who was experiencing a very upsetting crisis said, "You know, it feels as though I opened the doors of a blast furnace and the heat I'm experiencing is unbearable. I feel as though I'm melting away. There's going to be nothing left of me."

Sometimes life does feel that way in grief. However, one of the most effective principles of how to handle loss is found in the statement of three men who literally faced a furnace.

Nebuchadnezzar responded and said to them, "Is it true, Shadrach, Meshach and Abed-nego, that you do not serve my gods or worship the golden image that I have set up? Now if you are ready, at the moment you hear the sound of the horn, flute, lyre, trigon, psaltery and bagpipe and all kinds of music, to fall down and worship the image that I have made, very well. But if you do not worship, you will immediately be cast into the midst of a furnace of blazing fire; and what god is there who can deliver you out of my hands?"

Shadrach, Meshach and Abed-nego replied to the king, "O Nebuchadnezzar, we do not need to give you an answer concerning this matter. If it be so, our God whom we serve is able to deliver us from the furnace of blazing fire; and He will deliver us out of your hand, O king. But even if He does not, let it be known to you, O king, that we are not going to serve your gods or worship the golden image that you have set up" (Dan. 3:14-18, *NASB*).

Did you hear what they said? "Even if He does not." There it is—a statement of trust, faith, of living above and beyond the circumstances of life.

Each of us has our own dreams, desires, expectations and hopes for our life. If these come to pass, we say, "Everything is all right. I can handle life and I'm content. Now I can have the peace and stability I was looking for."

For many of us, our faith is dependent on getting God to do what we need, especially when we're deeply hurting. However, this is not the biblical pattern. It's all right to say, "Oh, I hope it turns out that way." "I hope the escrow doesn't fall through." "I hope he pulls through the operation." But we must also learn to say, "*It will be all right,* even if it doesn't turn out that way."

Our stability in life begins when we can say, "even if He does not." This is not a denial of life's problems. It is not rolling over and giving up or refusing to face life. It is a matter of surrendering to the wisdom of God, and through this we gain strength. But this is a process and it takes longer than most of us think it will when we're in grief.

Each of us has his or her own fiery furnace to face at one time or another. When losses hit, we must experience the normal emotional responses that are part of the healing process, and then, with God's strength and stability, face the results. God does come in and say, "Let's go through this together." Things will be better tomorrow, but better from God's perspective. Saying, "even if He doesn't" means that we are willing to leave the results to God.

It is God who gives us the grace to live life. Grace is God's assurance that life can be all right when everything in it is all wrong. It is the power to live life today as if things will be all right tomorrow. Lewis Smedes says it so well:

> Grace does not make everything right. Grace's trick is to show us that it is right for us to live; that it is truly good, wonderful even, for us to be breathing and feeling at the same time that everything

clustering around us is wholly wretched. Grace is not a ticket to Fantasy Island; Fantasy Island is dreamy fiction. Grace is not a potion to charm life to our liking; charms are magic. Grace does not cure all our concerns, transform all our kids into winners, or send us all soaring into the high skies of sex and success. Grace is rather an amazing power to look earthly reality in the face, see its sad and tragic edges, feel its cruel cuts, join in the primeval chorus against the outrageous unfairness, and yet feel in your deepest being that it is good and right for you to be alive and on God's good earth.[1]

The Positive Side of Grief

Losses hurt, but there is a positive side. Months or years after the loss, people are able to see how they grew and changed as a result of the situation.

Years ago, the Flying Wallenda family experienced a tragedy while performing at a circus. As they attempted to perform a difficult formation on the high wire, two members of the family were killed and two were injured for life.

For a while the Wallendas stopped their performances. They withdrew and became cautious, which was a normal response. In time, however, they said they would get back up on the wire once again. In fact, they would perform the very act that led to the tragedy.

The day came for the comeback. While people waited in the stands, the Wallendas successfully reconstructed their human pyramid on the high wire. After the performance, reporters descended upon them. "Why did you try this act again, after the tragedy?" The senior member of the family replied immediately, "To be on the wire is life. All else is waiting."

The question is, "How do you get back on the wire after a tragic fall?"[2] Your theology will affect how you respond to the death of a loved one. Your response will be determined by your understanding of God.

We are people who usually put faith in formulas. We feel comfortable with predictability, regularity and assurance. We want God to be like that as well, and so we try to create Him to be what we want Him to be and what we want Him to do. However, you and I cannot predict what God will do. Paul reminds us of that: "O the depth of the riches both of the wisdom and knowledge of God! how unsearchable are his judgments, and his ways past finding out!" (Rom. 11:33, *KJV*).

God isn't busy elsewhere. He is neither insensitive nor punitive. He is supreme, sovereign, loving and sensitive.

I don't fully comprehend God. I, too, have unanswered questions about some of the events of my life. Why was my son born so mentally challenged and with brain damage? I don't know and probably never will. But all of life's trials, problems, crises and suffering occur by divine permission. Don Baker wrote:

> God allows us to suffer. This may be the only solution to the problem that we will ever receive. Nothing can touch the Christian without having first received the

permission of God. If I do not accept that statement, then I really do not believe that God is sovereign—and if I do not believe in His sovereignty, then I am helpless before all the forces of heaven and hell.[3]

God allows suffering for His purpose and for His reasons. He gives the permission. This should help us see God as the gracious controller of the universe. God is free to do as He desires, and He doesn't have to give us explanations or share His reasons. He doesn't owe us. He has already given us His Son and His Holy Spirit, who strengthens and guides us. We look at problems and crises and say, "Why?" Jesus asks us to look at them and say, "Why not?"

What God allows us to experience is for our growth. God has arranged the seasons of nature to produce growth, and He arranges the experiences of the seasons of our lives for growth as well. Some days bring sunshine, and some bring storms. Both are necessary. He knows the amount of pressure we can handle. The apostle Paul tells us that

God will "not let you be tempted beyond what you can bear" (1 Cor. 10:13). But He does let us be tempted, feel pain, and experience suffering. He gives us not always what we think we need or want, but what will produce growth.

A woman came to me for counseling some time ago. She was in the midst of several losses, and she was upset because a friend had suggested she thank God for the problems she was experiencing.

"I can't believe she'd say that," the woman exclaimed. "That's ridiculous! It's insensitive! How can I thank God for being hurt?" She continued to vent her frustration.

After a while I said, "I wonder what she meant by her comment."

"What do you mean?" she replied.

"Well, did she mean to thank God for this time in your life as though it were good in and of itself—or to thank God for using the situation so that you can change and grow? Could that be it?"

"Well ... I don't know," she ventured.

"I know it hurts, and your family wishes it had never occurred," I said. "But it did. So the past can't be changed, and you feel out of control. Perhaps you can't change what happens in the future but you can control your response to whatever occurs. It's just something to think about."

She did think about it, and in time she came to the place of thanking God for being with her and allowing her this time of growth.

"One day I thought about the choices that I had," she said. "I could depend on God, thank Him and praise Him and allow Him to work through me. This didn't seem so bad to me when I considered the alternative!"

Growth Through Loss

What kind of growth can we expect? Lloyd Ogilvie suggests some of the things we can learn as we go through the difficult times in life, which he calls valleys:

> First, it has been in the valleys of waiting for answers to my prayers that I have made the

greatest strides in growing in the Lord's grace.

Second, it's usually in retrospect, after the strenuous period is over, that I can look back with gratitude for what I've received of the Lord Himself. I wouldn't trade the deeper trust and confidence I experienced from the valley for a smooth and trouble-free life.

Third, I long to be able to remember what the tough times provide in my relationship with the Lord, so that when new valleys occur, my first reaction will be to thank and praise the Lord in advance for what is going to happen in and through me as a result of what happens to me. I really want my first thought to be, "Lord, I know You didn't send this, but You have allowed it and will use it as a part of working all things together for good. I trust You completely, Lord!"[4]

This attitude doesn't negate the turmoil of our loss. When we are struggling with our pain, we feel like the disciples adrift in that small boat during the storm on the Sea of Galilee. The waves throw us about, and just as we get our legs under us, we're hit from another direction. The disciples struggled on the Sea of Galilee, and we struggle on the sea of life. All of us are afraid of capsizing. All we see are the waves that seem to grow each moment. We're afraid. Fear is the strong emotion of grief. However, Jesus came to the disciples and He comes to us today with the same message: "It is I; don't be afraid" (John 6:20). Do you remember the words of the song, "Here comes Jesus, walking on water, He'll lift you up..."?

> Here comes Jesus, see Him walking on the water,
> He'll lift you up and He'll help you to stand;
> Oh, here comes Jesus, He's the Master of the waves that roll,
> Here comes Jesus, He'll save your soul.
> Here comes Jesus, see Him walking on the water,
> He'll lift you up and He'll help you to stand;

Oh, here comes Jesus, He's the Master of the waves that roll,
Here comes Jesus, He'll make you whole.[5]

You ask God, "Where are You?" But He is there in the midst of your grief. You ask Him, "When? When will You answer?" just as the psalmist cried, "How long, O LORD? Will you forget me forever? How long will you hide your face from me? How long must I wrestle with my thoughts and every day have sorrow in my heart? How long will my enemy triumph over me?" (Ps. 13:1-2). We want Him to act according to our timetable, but the Scripture says, "Be still before the Lord and wait patiently for Him" (Ps. 37:7). We become restless in waiting. And to block out the pain of waiting, we are often driven into frantic activity. This does not help, however, but resting before the Lord does. As Larry Richards states:

> Often waiting is a time of darkening clouds. Our skies do not lighten. Instead, everything seems to become even more grim. Yet the darkening of our skies may forecast

the dawn. It is in the gathering folds of deepening shadows that God's hidden work for us takes place. The present, no matter how painful, is of utmost importance. Somewhere, where our eyes cannot see and our ears are unable to hear, God is. And God is at work.[6]

You may not feel that God is doing anything! Why? Because we want more results *now.* The instant-solution philosophy of our society often invades a proper perspective of God. We complain about waiting for a few weeks or days, but to God a day is as a thousand years and a thousand years is as an instant. God works in hidden ways even when you and I are totally frustrated by His apparent lack of response. We are just unaware that He is active. Hear the words of Isaiah for the people then and for us now:

> Since ancient times no one has heard,
> no ear has perceived,
> no eye has seen any God besides you,

> who acts on behalf of those who wait for him.
> You come to the help of those who gladly do right,
> who remember your ways (Isa. 64:4-5).

God has a reason for everything He does and a timetable for when he does it. "'For I know the plans I have for you,' declares the LORD, 'plans to prosper you and not to harm you, plans to give you hope and a future'" (Jer. 29:11). Give yourself permission not to know what, how and when. Even though you feel adrift, God is holding you and He knows the direction of your drift. Giving yourself permission to wait can give you hope. It is all right for God to ask us to wait for weeks and months and even years. It sometimes takes that long in grief. During that time when we do not receive the answer and/or solution we think we need, He gives us His presence. "But I trust in you, O LORD; I say, 'You are my God.' My times are in your hands" (Ps. 31:14-15).

There are some individuals who survive grief better than others and move ahead with their lives. Others become anchored in the tragedy and pain, and their growth is stunted. Some adults recover and go on with productive lives in spite of the tragedy of a sudden death or something else.

What is the difference? Who are the survivors?

How to Cope with and Survive Loss

Those who are able to survive a tragedy give credit to one person who ministered to them, stood by them and gave them hope. They reached out for help. Who do you have?

To help survive a crisis, you need the support of a friend. A friend helps you cope with your fears. Often we experience the fear of abandonment, but the presence of a friend reduces this. A friendship affirms that we won't be abandoned. A friend helps to break the hold of feelings of helplessness and hopelessness. Dr. Elton May says, "One friend, one person who is truly understanding, who takes the trouble to listen to us as we consider our problem, can change our whole outlook on the world."[7]

A second characteristic of those who survive is the ability to understand the extent of the loss. To recover, you need to fully experience the loss. Talking over the loss and letting tears drain is necessary. Denying it and its depth delays recovery. Facing it head-on helps you remember what you have lost but promotes healing.

Your pain and hurt do not go out the door of your life at one point in time. It is more of a slow drainage. And as there are seasons during the years, there are seasons of drainage. There is a season of sadness, a season of anger, a season of tranquility, a season of hope. These seasons do not always follow sequentially in a crisis. Winter, spring and summer can get jumbled together. One morning you may feel that hope and sunlight have entered your life again. But the next day, the storm is back. You smile one minute and cry the next.

A third characteristic of survivors is that they stop blaming themselves and stop living with guilt. Too often we ask "If only..." again and again, and "What have I done to deserve this?" Guilt weakens us and delays recovery more than any other factor. Our self-talk tends to become negative and we must make a conscious effort to be objective and self-affirming. Even when we are responsible for the occurrence, we must forgive ourselves. Because of our acceptance and forgiveness by God, we *can* forgive ourselves. (If you struggle with your self-talk you may want to read my book *A Better Way to Think* [Grand Rapids, MI: Baker Publishing Group, 2011].)

Survivors are those who have a purpose in life. They do not live in the past or focus on the negatives. In spite of the loss, they are willing to search out the positives that do exist in their lives. Expecting something more from life helps the recovery process. What is this element of expectation? Hope!

There is yet a final characteristic of those who not only survive but who also move forward as stronger individuals. It is the ability to develop a biblical perspective on life.

"Consider it all joy, my brethren, when you encounter various trials, knowing that the testing [or trying] of your faith produces endurance" (Jas. 1:2-3, *NASB*). It's easy to read a passage like this and say, "Well, that's fine." It is another thing, however, to put it into practice.

What does the word "consider" actually mean? It refers to an internal attitude of the heart of the mind that allows trials and circumstances of life to affect us either adversely or beneficially. Another way James 1:2 might be translated is, "Make up your mind to regard adversity as something to welcome or be glad about."

You have the power to decide what your attitude will be. You can approach it and say, "That's terrible. Totally upsetting. That is the last thing I wanted for my life. Why did it have to happen now? Why me?"

The other way of considering the same difficulty is to say, "It's not what I wanted or expected, but it's here. There are going to be some difficult times, but how can I make the best of them?" Don't ever deny the pain or the hurt that you might have to go through, but always ask, "What can I learn from it? How can I grow through this? How can it be used for God's glory?"

The verb tense used in the word "consider" indicates a decisiveness of action. It's not an attitude of resignation—"Well, I'll just give up. I'm just stuck with this problem. That's the way life is." If you resign yourself, you will sit back and not put forth any effort. The verb tense actually indicates that you will have to go against your natural inclination to see the trial as a negative force. There will be some moments when you won't see it like that at all, and then you'll have to remind yourself, "No, I think there is a better way of responding to this. Lord, I really want You to help me see it from a different perspective." And then your mind will shift to a more constructive response. This often takes a lot of work on your part.

God created us with both the capacity and the freedom to determine how we will respond to those unexpected incidents that life brings our way. You may honestly wish that a certain event had never occurred, but you cannot change the fact.

During the time of loss as well as the other times of life, our stability comes from our Lord. God's Word says:

> Now to Him who is able to establish you according to my gospel and the preaching of Jesus Christ, according to the revelation of the mystery which has been kept secret for long ages past (Rom. 16:25, *NASB*).

> Then he said to them, "Go eat of the fat, drink of the sweet, and send portions to him who has nothing prepared; for this day is holy to our Lord. Do not be grieved, for the joy of the LORD is your strength" (Neh. 8:10, *NASB*).

> And He will be the stability of your times, a wealth of salvation, wisdom, and knowledge; the fear of the LORD is his treasure (Isa. 33:6, *NASB*).

It hurts, but what can you do? What a tragedy if there is no way out! But there is a way out. This is the message of the Bible. *You can find courage for living with your losses.* Loss is the overture. Hurt is the introduction. Courage is the climax, and God is the ultimate resource.

This is the message of Job: "Though he [God] slay me, yet will I hope in him" (Job 13:15); or David: "Yea, though I walk through the valley of the shadow of death, I will fear no evil: for thou art with me; thy rod and thy staff they comfort me" (Ps. 23:4, *KJV*). This was the message of Isaiah: "Thou wilt keep him in perfect peace, whose mind is stayed on thee: because he trusteth in thee" (Isa. 26:3, *KJV*). This was the message of Paul: "For I am persuaded, that neither death, nor life, nor angels, nor principalities, nor powers, nor things present, nor things to come, Nor height, nor depth, nor any other creature, shall be able to separate us from the love of God, which is in Christ Jesus our Lord" (Rom. 8:38-39, *KJV*).

The three questions to ask in the middle of loss are:
1. What can I learn from this?
2. How can I grow through this?

3. How can God be glorified through this?

When you and I are afflicted and faint, we are invited to pour out our laments to the Lord. Gradually, as we do, the Holy Spirit will shift the focus of our awareness. He will lead us to remember the nature of the one to whom we speak. In remembering the Lord, our perspective will gradually change. The surging emotions will begin to still. The fears will quiet; the turbulence will give way to peace. As we remember who God is, our prayer will express trust, and we will find ourselves moved to praise.

11

Helping Others

In *Living a Life that Matters,* author Harold Kushner writes:
> At some of the darkest moments of my life,
> some people I thought of as friends deserted me—some
> because they cared about me and it
> hurt them to see me in pain; others because
> I reminded them of their own vulnerability,
> and that was more than they could handle.
> but real friends overcame their discomfort and
> came to sit with me. if they had no words to make me
> feel better, they sat in silence (much better than saying,
> "You'll get over it," or "It's not so bad;
> others have it worse"), and I loved them for it.[1]

There will come a time in all of our lives when we'll have an opportunity to minister to someone else, whether it is a friend, relative or neighbor, when they have lost a loved one. This is the calling God has given us:

> Praise be to the God and Father of our Lord Jesus Christ, the Father of compassion and the God of all comfort, who comforts us in all our troubles, so that we can comfort those in any trouble with the comfort we ourselves have received from God. For just as the sufferings of Christ flow over into our lives, so also through Christ our comfort overflows. If we are distressed, it is for your comfort and salvation; if we are comforted, it is for your comfort, which produces in you patient endurance of the same sufferings we suffer. And our hope for you is firm, because we know that just as you share in our sufferings, so also you share in our comfort (2 Cor. 1:3-7).

What you and I have learned from our own losses is never wasted, and it can be used to assist others.

There is an additional source of pain your friend will need to contend with—other people who make statements that hurt rather than console, hinder rather than comfort, and prolong the pain rather than relieve it: "If an enemy were insulting me, I could endure it; if a foe were raising himself against me, I could hide from him. But it is you, a man like myself, a companion, my close friend, with whom I once enjoyed sweet fellowship as we walked with the throng at the house of God" (Ps. 55:12-14).

These people are secondary wounders. They give unwanted and bad advice as well as improperly applied Scripture. They are all around us, even at church, and your friend won't be the first to experience this. Remember Job? Frederick Buechner states:

> [Job] had four well-meaning but insufferable friends who came over to cheer him up and try to explain [his suffering]. They said that anybody with enough sense to come in out of the rain knew that God was just. They said that anybody old enough to spell his own name

knew that since God was just, he made bad things happen to bad people and good things happen to good people. They said that such being the case, you didn't need a Harvard diploma to figure out that since bad things had happened to Job, then ipso facto he must have done something bad himself. But Job hadn't and he said so, and that's not all he said either, "Worthless physicians are you all," he said, "Oh that you would keep silent, and it would be your wisdom!" (Job 13:4-5, *ESV*). They were a bunch of theological quacks, in other words and the smartest thing they could do was shut up. But they were too busy explaining things to listen.[2]

But many hesitate in helping others. "I don't know what to do or say" is their main concern. It's true, most don't people don't know what to say because we live in a culture (church culture included) that doesn't address the subject of loss and grief or how to assist others.

When you're uncertain about how to help someone in grief, it is a bit frightening to take that step. I hope the material in this chapter will encourage you and leave you with the feeling that you can help others. You do know what to say and do. God calls all of us to help others, and we are more likely to do so if we have some guidelines and instructions.

Self-Talk Is Never the Best Talk

There are people in your church, at work or in your neighborhood who need your help. There are so many people who don't have anyone to assist them on an ongoing basis. If a grieving person has no one to help them, no one to talk with, they end up talking to themselves, and the advice and help they give isn't the best.

Much of this chapter is what I do to minister at a time of grief. It's not therapy or counseling. It's helping. It's being there and being a support to the person. When you hear about someone's loss, make yourself available. Reach out to the person. When you see them, if you don't know what to say, just say, "I wish I knew what to say, but I don't." That's honest and the person will appreciate it.

Sometimes running interference for the person is helpful, such as handling and screening phone calls, Facebook messages or putting a sign on the door limiting visiting time. Sometimes it helps to assist the person to identify who the people are they want around them and who the ones are they don't want around (the miserable comforters of Job type).

Because most individuals experiencing grief aren't informed about what to expect, they tend to believe they are going crazy. One of the most important ways to help a person in grief is to "normalize" what the person is experiencing. If you're starting from no knowledge about how to do this, don't do anything before you read this entire book. The information in these chapters can help you minister to others.

In chapter 1, "The World of Grief," you will find the listing of "Crazy Feelings of Grief." I share this with every person I work with, and it relieves them of their concerns. It gives them perspective on what they are experiencing and educates them about their journey of grief.

Someone you minister to may need your support for months or even years. One of the concerns of those in grief is that they will be forgotten, and so will their loved one. Whenever you talk about the deceased, be sure to use that person's name. Those in grief are fearful that their loved one will be forgotten and they appreciate hearing their name.

When you ask, "How are you doing?" and you hear, "Oh, fine" or "All right," it may be helpful to then ask, "But, how are you *really* doing?" to let them know you really want to hear and are truly concerned.

One way to minister to a neighbor or someone you don't know well is to wait and call about two months after the service. By now, most of their support has left and they may feel abandoned. Offer to bring over dinner and give them some choices for the meal. Mention that you will also bring the DVD *Tear Soup,* a 17-minute presentation that describes the grieving process clearly and can be used by the entire family.

I have used this DVD for years, and it quickly normalizes the grief process. When you go to the home with the food and DVD, and you sit and watch with them, you don't have to be concerned about being an expert on grief, for *Tear Soup* is very thorough and effective. Many who reach out in this way find that they return home with empty dishes but not with the DVD. Often the family requests that you leave *Tear Soup* with them for a while so they can view it again as well as show it to other family members and relatives.

The Gift of Listening

If you want to help your friend in grief, just be there. Your presence does wonders. If you want to help another person, just listen. One of the greatest gifts one person can give another is the gift of listening. It can be an act of love and caring like no other. But far too many people in conversation only *hear* one another. Few actually *listen.*

He who answers before listening—that is folly and shame (Prov. 18:13).

Let every man be quick to hear [a ready listener] (Jas. 1:19, *AMP*).

Listening means you're not thinking about what you're going to say when the other person stops talking. You are not busy formulating your response. You're concentrating on what is being said.

Listening means that you're completely accepting of what is being said, without judging what your friend is saying or how he or she is saying it. If you don't like your friend's tone of voice, or you can't condone what he or she is doing, and you react on the spot, you may miss the meaning of what your friend is saying. Acceptance doesn't mean that you agree with the content of what a person says; it means you acknowledge and understand that what the person is saying is something he or she is feeling.

Listening means being able to repeat what your friend has said and express what you think he or she is feeling while speaking to you. Real listening implies having a sincere interest in the other's feelings and opinions and attempting to understand those feelings from his or her perspective.

The word "hear" in the New Testament does not refer to an auditory experience. In most cases it means to *pay heed.* It requires tuning in to the right frequency.

Because of my disabled son, Matthew, who didn't have a vocabulary, I learned to listen with my eyes, reading the message in his nonverbal signals. This translated to my listening to what my counselees could not put into words. I learned to listen to the message behind the message—hurt, ache, frustration, loss of hope, fear of rejection, feelings of betrayal, joy, delight and the promise of change.

I also learned to reflect upon what I saw on another's face and in the person's posture, walk and pace. Then I shared with the person what I saw. This provided an opportunity to explain further what he or she was thinking and feeling. The person knew I was tuned in. Your friend needs to sense that you're in sync with him or her. Listen with your eyes to what he or she can't put into words.

Every message your friend shares has three parts: (1) the actual content, (2) the tone of voice, and (3) the nonverbal communication. It's possible to use the same word, statement or question to express many different messages simply by changing tone or voice or body movement. Nonverbal communication includes facial expression, body posture and gestures or actions.

It's been suggested that successful communication consists of 7 percent content, 38 percent tone of voice, and 55 percent nonverbal communication. We're usually aware of the content of what we're saying but not nearly as aware of our tone of voice.

When you say with the proper tone of voice, "I want to hear what you have to say," but then you bury your head in paper work or check your watch, what is your friend to believe? When you ask, "How was your day?" in a flat tone while walking by him, what does he respond to—the verbal or nonverbal message?

Some people listen for facts, information and details for their own use. Others listen because they feel sorry for the person. Your friend doesn't need this. On occasion, people listen out of obligation or necessity, or to be polite. If you do, your friend will pick up on it. Some who listen are nothing more than voyeurs who have an incessant need to pry and probe into other people's lives. But some listen *because they care,* and this kind of listening provides unlimited opportunities for real ministry in people's lives. Listening that springs from caring builds closeness, reflects love and is an act of grace. And this is what Jesus calls us to do.

You can listen even when the other person is not talking. Sometimes she's not able to talk, but your attentive presence lets your friend know you're there to listen. You let her know you want to hear her story when she's up to talking about it.

If your friend is devastated and coming apart at the seams, or sitting there stunned, you can't make her feel better or fix her. When we try it's often to help us feel useful and relieve our anxiety about seeing someone in this state. Remember, you can never be all you want to be or all that your friend wants you to be for her. Just sit with her and be there.

At times, you will be hurt, since some of what you offer or do will be rejected. Because you haven't experienced the same loss, she may feel uncomfortable with you while at the same time she wants your help. In your heart and mind, give her permission not to be as she was before her need. If something is said or done that offends you, remind yourself that your friend cannot be expected to be as she was. You may wonder, *Did I say something wrong? Am I off base?* The answer is no. You're dealing with unpredictability. You're all right.

You may be tempted at times to set your friend straight spiritually. You might hear statements like, "I thought I could count on God, but even He let me down" or "How could a loving God let something like that happen?" or "I think I'm losing my faith in God. I can't even pray anymore." Squelch your desire to start quoting Bible verses, shove a book in the person's face or try to give answers. Be glad you're hearing where she is spiritually at this moment in time. Respond with a simple, "Yes, what's happened doesn't make much sense, does it? It's hard to understand. I wish I had an answer for you." Or just listen and reflect.

There will be times when your friend doesn't want you around. If you sense that might be the case, ask her, "What would be more comfortable for you at this time: for me to be here with you or to give you some space? I can do either." If your presence isn't needed, say, "I'll check back with you another time to see what I can do to assist you."

The best support you can give your friend is to *normalize her feelings.* This simply means reassuring her that what she is experiencing is natural; she isn't crazy. This advice can provide the greatest relief of all. But it means *you* need to understand what someone experiences from losing a family member.

How can you help someone else? There are many elements involved. In Proverbs 3:5-6, we are instructed to "Lean on, trust in, and be confident in the Lord with all your heart and mind and do not rely on your own insight or understanding. In all your ways know, recognize, and acknowledge Him, and he will direct and make straight and plain your paths" *(AMP).*

With all their years of training and experience, professional counselors frequently wonder what they should do or say. This experience prompts all of us to go back to the Lord and ask, "Lord, what should I do now? What does this person need?" You'll find yourself there time and time again. If you begin to assist and help your friend out of your own strength, you'll make mistakes. We all need to rely upon the power and wisdom of God.

Be Genuine in Your Offer to Help

Helping others includes experiencing genuine interest and love for the individual. We can listen, and we can rely upon the power of God for knowing how to respond, but we must also have a genuine interest and love for the person. If it's not there, you can't fake it, and your friend will know if you are. "Oil and perfume rejoice the heart; so does the sweetness of a friend's counsel that comes from the heart" (Prov. 27:9, AMP). It's so easy to rattle off an answer that's superficial and doesn't meet your friend's need. We have to ask ourselves, *How do I really feel about helping this person? Am I genuinely concerned? If not, maybe I should pray about my own attitude. Perhaps I'm not the one to try to help.* You will be drawn to help some and not help others. It could be that their problems are beyond you; maybe they overwhelm you or activate some unresolved issues in your own life.

Well-Timed and Well-Chosen Words

To help someone, you need to know when to speak and when enough has been said. Proverbs 10:19 emphasizes this principle: "In a multitude of words transgression is not lacking, but he who restrains his lips is prudent" *(AMP)*. This is a sign of an individual who has knowledge. He chooses his words well. "Even fools seem to be wise if they keep quiet; if they don't speak, they appear to understand" (Prov. 17:28, *NCV*).

Watch the way you talk. Let nothing foul or dirty come out of your mouth. Say only what helps, each *word* a *gift* (Eph. 4:29, *THE MESSAGE,* emphasis added).

Do you see a man who is hasty in his words? There is more hope for a [self-confident] fool than for him (Prov. 29:20, *AMP*).

Being hasty means you just go ahead and blurt out what you're thinking without considering the effect it will have on others. If you're an extrovert, you probably need to talk to think something through. Extroverts tend to talk first and then realize what they've said. But this is a time to hold back and get your thoughts in order. When you are ministering to a hurting friend, and she shares something that shocks you, don't feel that you have to respond immediately. I've heard people respond to their hurting friend, "You did *what?*" Don't do that. Take a few moments to pray, asking God to give you the words. Then try to formulate what you want to say.

If you don't know what to say, one of the best things to do is ask for more information: "Tell me some more about it" or "Give me some more background." This gives you more time. You don't have to come right out and say something. There may be times when you say, "I need a few seconds to go through what you said and decide what to share at this time." This takes the pressure off of you and also off of your friend.

Timing is another important principle. "A man has joy in making an apt answer, and a word spoken at the right moment—how good it is!" (Prov. 15:23, *AMP*). The correct answer spoken at the right moment is what is needed. Wait. Silence is not bad.

Keeping confidences is foundational. Can you keep a confidence when somebody shares something with you? "Gossips can't keep secrets, so avoid people who talk too much" (Prov. 20:19, *NCV*). If you have a friend who is a gossiper, who can't keep something hidden, the Scripture is saying, watch out! Don't associate with that person too much. "He who guards his mouth and his tongue keeps himself from troubles" (Prov. 21:23, *AMP*).

Most of us, when we've had something shared with us, have been tempted to share it with others—even a confidence from a friend. And the more shocking it is, the more we're tempted to share. But each conversation is a violation of trust, and a tremendous damage is done to friendship by sharing confidences. What you must do as a Christian and as a friend is to ask God to help you bury confidential information deep inside or give it away to the Lord so that it will not come out, either on purpose or through some subconscious motivation.

There are times when I have asked God to help me forget what I have heard. Does your friend want you to share this issue with anyone else, including family? Ask her. (If she's highly suicidal or homicidal, you will have to get some assistance.)

Another Scripture passage reflects the idea of sensitive understanding: "Singing songs to someone who is sad is like taking away his coat on a cold day or pouring vinegar on soda" (Prov. 25:20, *NCV*). Being merry and joyful around the person who is deeply hurting and suffering, and making inappropriate comments or jokes, even statements such as, "Oh, you really don't feel that way; snap out of it," is inappropriate. Your friend hurts so much that she's unable to focus on what is happening. And such inappropriate statements or jokes can add to her pain. You need to be sensitive.

Gentle Confrontation

So how do you give good advice? Make suggestions tentatively: "What if you did...?" "Have you ever considered...?" "What possibilities have you come up with?" It's safest when giving advice to offer several alternatives. Don't say to a person, "This is exactly what you need to do."

If you do, you are assuming the responsibility for the solution. If your suggestion doesn't work, she may come back and say, "You really gave me a stupid idea. It didn't work. It's your fault." Giving several tentative suggestions not only is safer for you but also enables your friend to think it through for herself. Most people have the ability to resolve their problems, but they need the encouragement to do it.

Speak Without Judgment

Gently raise some questions when you see a friend headed down the wrong path. This is not an attack on another person if given gently and sensitively. Gentleness is important, because she may already be feeling guilty and ashamed, and experiencing what she sees as judgment or condemnation will likely make her feel rejected.

Confront someone only when you have genuine empathy for her. A confrontation should be an act of grace. It's done to reveal discrepancies or distortions in someone's direction or thinking. Confrontation is also used to challenge a friend's underdeveloped and unused skills and resources.

Your purpose in confronting your friend should be to help her make better decisions for herself, to become more accepting of where she is in life and to be more productive and less self-destructive. "Wounds from a friend can be trusted, but an enemy multiplies kisses" (Prov. 27:6).

You cannot use the same approach for every person; you must be sensitive to individual needs. Adaptability is important: "And we earnestly beseech you, brethren, admonish (warn and seriously advise) those who are out of line ... encourage the timid and fainthearted, help and give your support to the weak souls, [and] be very patient with everybody [always keeping your temper]" (1 Thess. 5:14, *AMP*).

Whenever you confront, don't do it out of anger or by making a statement. You may wish you could point out that what someone is doing is irresponsible or even dumb, but you would offend and possibly even sever the relationship.

Your friend needs to hear care, love and concern in your voice, where confrontation is accomplished with questions such as, "I wonder if..." "Could it be...?" "Is it possible...?" "Does this make sense to you?" and "How do you react to this perception?" With your questions, *lead* her to where you want her to go. Practice these questions out loud again and again until they're a part of your helping reservoir of information and approach.

Speak Words that Build

Another principle we find in the Word of God is edification. Some of these passages might be familiar to you. Galatians 6:2 teaches the concept of bearing one another's burdens. Romans 14:19 reads, "So let us then aim for and eagerly pursue ... mutual upbuilding (edification and development) of one another" *(AMP).* The word "edify," which is part of helping, means to hold up or to promote growth in Christian wisdom, grace, virtue and holiness. Our helping includes edification. To know if your speech is edifying, you must ask yourself, "Is what I'm sharing with that person going to cause her to grow in the Christian life and assist her to be strong?" "Will this help my friend with his loss and grief?" A friend might come to you and say, "I really want you to help me." But what does she mean by *help?* She might mean agreeing with her point of view or even taking her side. That is where you get into difficulty.

Speak Words that Encourage

Another way of helping others is encouragement: "Anxiety in a man's heart weighs it down, but an encouraging word makes it glad" (Prov. 12:25, *AMP*); "Therefore encourage (admonish, exhort) one another and edify (strengthen and build up) one another, just as you are doing" (1 Thess. 5:11, *AMP*).

The *American Heritage Dictionary* offers one of the better definitions of "encourage." It's a "tendency or disposition to expect the best possible outcome, or to dwell on the most helpful aspect of a situation." When this is your attitude or perspective, you'll be able to encourage others. Encouragement is recognizing the other person as having worth and dignity. It means paying attention to her when she is sharing with you.

"Let us encourage one another" (Heb. 10:25). The word here means to keep someone on her feet who, if left to herself, would collapse. Your encouragement serves like the concrete pilings of a structural support.

Speak from True Understanding

Involvement and empathy are the scriptural basis for helping. Empathy is one of the most important commodities for helping others. It means viewing the situation through your friend's eyes, feeling as she feels. The scriptural admonition to bear one another's burdens in Galatians 6:2 and to rejoice with those who rejoice and weep with those who weep, in Romans 12:15, is what we call empathy.

It involves discrimination—to be able to get inside the other person, to look at the world through her perspective or frame of reference, and to get a feeling for what her world is like. Not only is it the ability to discriminate, but also to communicate to your friend this understanding in such a manner that she realizes you have picked up her feelings and behavior. We must be able to see with another person's eyes what their world is like. It is like being able to see another person's joy, to understand what underlies that joy and to communicate this understanding to the person. Can you do this? Yes, you can learn. Be patient with yourself and with others.

What to Say and Not to Say

There are many responses to share that are helpful; but there are also many responses that will wound a person who is grieving the loss of a loved one. Here are examples of what *not* to say as well as responses that can be helpful.

God Clichés

It was God's will.
This will make your faith stronger.
God needs him/her more than you do.
God has a reason for this.
Only the good die young.
God never gives us more than we can handle.

Unhealthy Expectations

Be grateful that you still have your (can have) other children.
Aren't you lucky that at least...
You must be strong for your (other) children, spouse, and so on.
You must get hold of yourself.
Don't take it so hard.
You'll get over this.
You must focus on your precious memories.
You have to keep busy.

Ignorance

Let's not talk about it.
She died because...

It must have been his/her time to go.
Things always work out for the best.
Something good always comes out of tragedy.
You're not the only one who suffers.

Basic Insensitivity

I know just how you feel. My _____ died last year.
She never knew what hit her.
Time heals all wounds.
She had a very full life.
It could have been worse if...
Let me know if there's anything I can do.

Helpful Phrases

I can't imagine how difficult this is for you.
I know this is very painful for you.
I'm so sorry for your loss of ... (inclusive, rather than pitying).
It's harder than most people think.
It's a normal response to be angry with God.
It must be hard to accept.

How can I be of help?
Let's spend some time together.
People really cared for him/her.
I'm praying for you and wondered how you would like me to pray.
You are not alone; I'm here to help.
I know this must feel like a dream to you.
Tell me how you're feeling.
From what you said, I know you will miss him/her.
I'd give anything to be able to make it better for you, but I know that I can't.
Most people who have gone through this react just as you are.
Tell me about (deceased's name) and your life with him/her.
May I just sit here with you?
Is there anyone I can call for you?
I'll call you tomorrow. In the meantime, if you need me, here is my phone number.[3]

The Timing of Handwritten Notes

If there is anything that helps a hurting person more than spoken words it is the written expressions of comfort. Following the death of our son, we received so many written expressions from people. And this went on for more than 12 years—that's what helped so much. But while *we* continued to receive written words of comfort, most people don't.

Most who are hurting receive an abundance of cards and notes at first, during a time when their pain is so great the words of comfort may not register as much as they will later on. Write reminders on your calendar to *send notes every three to four months for at least two years.* All it takes is one person dong this; your act of caring sends the message, "Your loss is not forgotten." And remember, losses are not confined to deaths.

Perhaps the most important part of sending a note is to put it in your own handwriting. A typed note, text, email or card purchased that you only sign doesn't convey the same message as one in your own handwriting. Many letters that you write will be kept and reread for years.

Writing letters and notes to a hurting friend is not easy. In fact, for many the most challenging letter to write is a letter of condolence. How can you craft a simple expression of words on a page that can penetrate the pain of loss and grief and bring support and care to a friend's heart and mind? We don't want to be superficial or stilted in our expression. So it's easy to postpone writing to the extent that we never do it, even though we wanted to reach out in this way.

What to Include in a Condolence Note or Letter

Listen to your feelings of compassion and care, then simply translate those feelings into your own words. Here are some specific suggestions that may help you.

The first component of a letter is to *acknowledge* the loss. If someone other than your friend informed you, let him know how you learned about his loss. It's all right to express your feelings about hearing of the loss.

Express your *concern.* Let your friend know that you care and in some way connect with his sense of loss. If you know the person who died (or left or otherwise was involved in your friend's loss), share your sadness. And use the appropriate words.

It helps to make a note of *special qualities of the person who died.* This can be done whether you knew him personally or just through the stories of your friend. In doing this, you're reminding your friend that the person he lost made a contribution and was appreciated.

It helps to *share a special memory* you have of the one who died. This can help your friend, since his shocked grief has short-circuited his ability to remember details.

In addition to memories, it's helpful to *maintain special qualities about your friend.* This is a time when he is so overwhelmed that he may question his own capabilities. Bring out any traits that helped him deal with past adversities. As the months go by, send another note and say that you were thinking about him, praying for him and remembering.

How to Pray with Those in Grief

Sometimes I ask people exactly what they would like me to pray about and allow them to direct me. On other occasions I say, "This is how I'm going to pray for you this week." There will be times when this is what keeps your friend going. And before you give this request to others or put it on a prayer chain, find out if this is all right with him. It's a way of asking, "Who do you want to know about this?"

As you pray, rely on the Holy Spirit for instruction in how to pray. Allow Him to bring to mind through your imagination the direction needed in prayer. Too often we quickly pray with our own words, which come from our intellect. Our prayer lacks freshness because it reflects our own direction and not that of the Holy Spirit.

Be careful about asking your friend to pray. He may be angry at God or just doesn't have the words at this time. As J. Rupp notes, "Grief has a way of plundering our prayer life, leaving us feeling immobile and empty."[4]

Ask your friend if he would like you to pray with him or for him. Don't be intrusive and don't pray long! Keep it brief and sensitive. If you have the opportunity to pray for someone in the midst of deep difficulty, see it as a privilege. I have seen some who pray because they either don't know what to say or they're uncomfortable with silence. And some pray trying to fix or to spiritually convict their friend. But your motivation should be to *bring your friend to God and His resources.*

Here are two examples of prayers:

O Lord, we have experienced a great tragedy and wrong. We are suffering and grieving over our pain and loss. Please help us. Please come and comfort us in our heartache and grief. Give us wisdom to know how to help one another through this crisis. Give us strength to do the practical things that are necessary. Give us discernment to help each other in our personal and corporate suffering. Give us renewed faith to trust in You. And give us hope that we may be vessels of Your goodness and mercy as we wait upon You. Amen.[5]

Father, we come today as confused and brokenhearted children. We don't understand, but we do trust You and know that You are still in control. We cannot change the past, but we do need strength for today and hope for the future. We know You see our sorrow, and we remember that Jesus wept. We're thankful that He is here with us to heal the brokenhearted. You know the feeling of shock that we have experienced, and You have promised to meet our needs.

Be open to God's leading, and may the words of Father Mychal Judge, a man who gave his life for others on 9/11, guide you:

Lord, take me where You want me to go,

Let me meet whom You want me to meet.

Help me to say what You want me to say.
And keep me from getting in Your way!

Endnotes

Introduction

[1] Thomas Attig, *How We Grieve* (New York: Oxford University Press, 1996), p.171.

Chapter 1: The World of Grief

[1] Gregory Floyd, *A Grief Unveiled* (Brewster, MA: Paraclete Press, 1999), pp.116-117.
[2] Doug Manning, *Don't Take My Grief Away from Me* (Sevierville, TN: Insight Publishing, 2005), p.41.
[3] Gerald Sittser, *A Grace Disguised* (Grand Rapids, MI: Zondervan, 1996), p.47.
[4] Anne Morrow-Lindberg, *Camp's Unfamiliar Quotations* (New York: Prentice Hall, 1990), p.124.
[5] Therese A. Rando, *How to Go on Living When Someone You Love Dies* (New York: Bantam, 1991).

[6] Joanne T. Jozefowski, *The Phoenix Phenomenon* (Northvale, NJ: Jason Aronson, Inc. 2001), p.17.
[7] Judy Tatelbaum, *The Courage to Grieve* (New York: Perennial, 1980), p.28.
[8] Ken Gire, *The Weathering Grace of God* (Ann Arbor, MI: Servant Publications, 2001), p.109.
[9] Linda Schupp, Ph.D., *Assessing and Treating Trauma* (Eau Claire, WI: DESI, 2004), p.3.
[10] Thomas Attig, *The Heart of Grief* (New York: Oxford University Press, 2000), p.xi.
[11] Ibid., pp.xii, xvi.
[12] J. Ship Jeffreys, *Helping Grieving People* (New York: Brunner-Rutledge, 2005), adapted, pp.31-40.
[13] Nancy Guthrie, *When Your Family's Lost a Loved One* (Wheaton, IL: Tyndale House, 2008), p.5.
[14] Ibid., adapted, p.3.
[15] Manning, *Don't Take My Grief Away from Me,* pp.66-67.

[16] Michael Leuing, *A Common Prayer* (New York: HarperCollins, 1991).

Chapter 2: The Loss of a Spouse

[1] William Wallace, *Living Again* (Lenexa, KS: Addax Publishing Group, 1998), pp.12-13.
[2] Joann T. Jozefowski, *The Phoenix Phenomenon* (Northvale, NJ: Jason Aronson, 1999), adapted, p.9.
[3] R. Scott Sullender, *Losses in Later Life* (New York: Paulist Press, 1989), adapted, p.115.
[4] Wallace, *Living Again,* adapted, p.139.
[5] Gay Hendricks, *Learning to Love Yourself,* quoted in Pamela Blair and Brook Noel, *I Wasn't Ready to Say Goodbye* (Naperville, IL: Sourcebook, Inc., 2008), pp.75-76.
[6] Ibid., p.47.
[7] Wallace, *Living Again,* adapted, p.130.
[8] Ibid., adapted, pp.70-71.
[9] Susan J. Zonnebelt-Smeenge, R.N., Ed.D., and Robert C.

DeVries, D.Min., Ph.D., *Getting in the Order Side of Grief* (Grand Rapids, MI: Baker Books, 2006), adapted, pp.66-67.

[10] John James and Frank Cherry, *The Grief Recovery Handbook* (New York: Harper and Row, 1988), adapted, pp.152-153.

[11] Therese A. Rando, Ph.D., *Grieving: How to Go on Living When Someone You Love Dies* (Lexington, MA: Lexington Books, 1988), adapted, p.251.

[12] Wallace, *Living Again,* adapted, p.131.

[13] Used by permission of the writer.

Chapter 3: The Death of a Child

[1] J. Ship Jeffreys, *Helping Grieving People* (New York: Brunner-Rutledge, 2005).

[2] Carol Staudacher, *Beyond Grief* (Oakland, CA: New Harbinger, 1987), adapted, pp.100-101.

[3] Therese A. Rando, *Grieving* (Lexington, MA: Lexington Books, 1989), pp.164-165.

[4] Ibid., adapted, p.105.
[5] Ibid., p.13.
[6] Theresa Huntley, *When Your Child Dies* (Minneapolis, MN: Augsburg, 2001), adapted, p.5.
[7] Ronald J. Knapp, *Beyond Endurance—When a Child Dies* (New York: Schocken, 1986), p.45.
[8] Ibid., pp.52-53.
[9] Staudacher, *Beyond Grief,* adapted, p.109.
[10] Catherine M. Sanders, Ph.D., *How to Survive the Loss of a Child* (Rocklin, CA: Prima Publishers), adapted, pp.69-74.
[11] Tom Easthope, CDE, "Grandparent's Grief Nipped in the Bud," *The Forum,* January/February/March 2003.
[12] Ibid., adapted.
[13] Mary Lou Reed, *Grandparents Cry Twice: Help for Bereaved Grandparents* (Amityville, NY: Baywood Publishing, 2000).
[14] Material adapted from Mary Lou Reed, "Grandparents Grief—Who Is Listening?" *The Forum,* January/February/March 2003

and *Grandparents Cry Twice: Help for Bereaved Grandparents* (Amityville, NY: Baywood Publishing Company, 2000).
[15] Staudacher, *Beyond Grief,* adapted, p.113.
[16] Knapp, *Beyond Endurance—When a Child Dies,* adapted, p.103.
[17] Ibid., p.41.
[18] Glen Davidson, *Understanding Mourning* (Minneapolis, MN: Augsburg, 1984), p.49.
[19] J. Shep Jeffreys, *Helping Grieving People* (New York: Brunner-Rutledge, 2005), p.125.
[20] Theresa Huntley, *When Your Child Dies* (Minneapolis, MN: Augsburg, 2001), pp.13-14.
[21] H. Norman Wright, *Recovering from the Losses of Life* (Grand Rapids, MI: Baker Books, 2006), adapted, pp.48-49.
[22] Knapp, *Beyond Endurance—When a Child Dies,* adapted, p.184.
[23] Ann Kaiser Stearns, *Coming Back* (New York: Ballantine, 1988), p.172.
[24] Knapp, *Beyond Endurance—When a Child Dies,* p.29.

[25] Rando, *Grieving,* adapted, p.169; Staudacher, *Beyond Grief,* adapted, p.116.
[26] Staudacher, *Beyond Grief,* adapted, pp.117-118.
[27] Rando, *Grieving,* adapted, pp.177-178.
[28] David W. Wiersbe, *Gone But Not Lost* (Grand Rapids, MI: Baker Books, 1992), p.55.
[29] Knapp, *Beyond Endurance—When a Child Dies,* p.206.
[30] Max Lucado, *The Applause of Heaven* (Dallas, TX: Word, 1990), pp.186-187.
[31] Ibid., p.190.

Chapter 4: Helping Children in Grief

[1] Mary Ann Emswiler, M.A., M.P.S., and James P. Emswiler, M.A., M.Ed, *Guiding Your Child Through Grief* (New York: Bantam Books, 2000), adapted, pp.100-106.
[2] Carol Staudacher, *Beyond Grief* (Oakland, CA: New Harbinger, 1987), pp.129-130.

[3] William Van Ornum and John B. Mordock, *Crisis Counseling with Children and Adolescents: A Guide for Nonprofessional Counselors* (New York: Continuum, 1983), adapted, pp.21-33.

[4] Dan Schaefer and Christine Lyons, *How Do We Tell the Children?* (New York: New Market Press, 1986), adapted, p.122.

[5] Ibid., p.129.

[6] Staudacher, *Beyond Grief,* pp.131-138.

[7] J. William Worden, *Children and Grief: When a Parent Dies* (New York: Guilford Press, 1996), pp.33-34.

[8] Schaefer and Lyons, *How Do We Tell the Children?* pp.33-34.

[9] Worden, *Children and Grief: When a Parent Dies,* pp.33-34.

[10] Schaefer and Lyons, *How Do We Tell the Children?* pp.124-125.

[11] Staudacher, *Beyond Grief,* pp.146-147.

[12] Helen Fitzgerald, *The Grieving Child* (New York: Simon and Schuster, 1992), p.106.

[13] Staudacher, *Beyond Grief,* p.151.

[14] Therese A. Rando, *Grieving: How to Go on Living When Someone You Love Dies* (Lexington, MA: Lexington Books, 1988), p.218.
[15] Schaefer and Lyons, *How Do We Tell the Children?* p.142.
[16] Rando, *Grieving: How to Go on Living When Someone You Love Dies,* p.218.

Chapter 5: The Death of a Parent

[1] Alexander Levy, *The Orphaned Adult* (Cambridge, MA: Da Capo Press, 2000), p.7.
[2] Lois F. Akner and Catherine Whitney, *How to Survive the Loss of a Parent* (Quill, NY: William Morrow 1993), adapted, pp.7-69.
[3] Therese A. Rando, *Grieving: How to Go on Living When Someone You Love Dies* (Lexington, MA: Lexington Books, 1988), adapted, pp.136-150.
[4] Rando, *Grieving: How to Go on Living When Someone You Love Dies,* p.143.

[5] Akner and Whitney, *How to Survive the Loss of a Parent,* p.141.
[6] Ibid., p.143.
[7] Ibid., adapted, pp.151-156.
[8] Ibid., adapted, pp.176-178.
[9] Levy, *The Orphaned Adult,* p.53.
[10] Jane Brooks, *Midlife Orphan* (New York: Berkley Trade, 1999), p.61.
[11] Ibid., pp.67,70.
[12] Akner and Whitney, *How to Survive the Loss of a Parent,* adapted, pp.110-111.

Chapter 6: Parent Loss—A Woman and Her Mother; A Man and His Father

[1] Therese Rando, *Grieving: How to Go on Living When Someone You Love Dies* (Lexington, MA: Lexington Books, 1988), adapted pp.142-144.
[2] Ibid., adapted, pp.142-146.
[3] Ibid., p.146.

[4] Hope Edelman, *Letters from Motherless Daughters* (New York: Delta, 1995), pp.24-25.

[5] Patricia Commins, *Remembering Mother, Finding Myself* (Deerfield Beach, FL: Health Communications, Inc., 1999), pp.54-55.

[6] Fiona Marshall, *Losing a Parent* (Cambridge Center, MA: Fisher Books, 1993), p.5.

[7] Harold Ivan Smith, *Grieving the Loss of a Mother* (Minneapolis, MN: Augsburg Books, 2003), p.4.

[8] Ibid., p.1.

[9] Marshall, *Losing a Parent,* p.45.

[10] Ibid., pp.66-67.

[11] Diane Hambrook and Gail Eisenberg with Herma M. Rosenthal, *A Mother Loss Workbook* (New York: Harper Perennial, 1997), adapted, pp.97-98.

[12] Judith Balswick, *Mothers and Daughters Making Peace* (Ann Arbor, MI: Servant Publications, 1993), adapted, p.213.

[13] Dave Veerman and Bruce Barton, *When Your Father Dies*

(Nashville, TN: Thomas Nelson, 2003), adapted, pp.55-70.
[14] Elizabeth Levang, *When Men Grieve* (Minneapolis, MN: Fairview Press, 1998), p.46.
[15] John Trent, quoted in Veerman and Barton, *When Your Father Dies,* p.9.
[16] Ibid., p.108.
[17] Ibid., p.109.
[18] John Ashcroft, *Lessons from a Father to a Son* (Nashville, TN: Thomas Nelson, 1998), p.201.
[19] Veerman and Barton, *When Your Father Dies,* adapted, pp.112-123.
[20] Ann Kaiser Stearns, *Living Through Personal Crisis* (New York: Ballantine Books, 1984), adapted, pp.65-66.
[21] Tom Golden, "Gender Differences in Grief," *Bereavement—A Magazine of Hope and Healing,* 9 (May/June 1995), adapted, p.7.
[22] Carol Staudacher, *Men and Grief* (Oakland, CA: New Harbinger Publications, 1991), adapted, pp.19-38.

Chapter 7: The Loss of a Sibling

[1] Pamela Blair and Brook Noel, *I Wasn't Ready to Say Goodbye* (Naperville, IL: Sourcebook, Inc., 2008), adapted, p.164.
[2] Marion Sandmaier, *Original Kin* (New York: E.P. Dutton, 1994), adapted, pp.207,214.
[3] Elizabeth DeVita Raeburn, *The Empty Room* (New York: Scribner, 2004), p.121.
[4] T.J. Wray, *Surviving the Death of a Sibling* (New York: Three Rivers Press, 2001), adapted, pp.146-158.
[5] Ibid., adapted, pp.161-164.
[6] Blair and Noel, *I Wasn't Ready to Say Goodbye,* p.166.
[7] Therese A. Rando, *Grieving: How to Go on Living When Someone You Love Dies* (Lexington, MA: Lexington Books, 1988), adapted, pp.154-158.
[8] Ibid., adapted, pp.155-159.
[9] Sandmaier, *Original Kin,* p.224.

[10] Janice Harris Lord, *No Time for Good Byes* (Burnesville, NC: Compassion Press, 2006), pp.84-85.

Chapter 8: The Loss of a Friend

[1] Dr. Archibald Hart, *Fifteen Principles for Achieving Happiness* (Waco, TX: Word Publishers, 1988), adapted, p.150.
[2] Ibid., p.15.
[3] Helen Fitzgerald, *The Mourning Handbook* (New York: Simon & Schuster, 1994), p.138.
[4] Harold Ivan Smith, *Friendgrief: An Absence Called Presence* (Amityville, NY: Baywood Publishing Company, 2001), pp.68-69.
[5] Louis F. Kavar, *Living with Loss* (Gaithersburg, MD: Chi Rio Press, 1991), p.12.
[6] Harold Ivan Smith, *Grieving the Death of a Friend* (Minneapolis, MN: Augsburg Press, 1996), adapted, pp.20-21.

[7] Pamela Blair and Brook Noel, *I Wasn't Ready to Say Goodbye* (Naperville, IL: Sourcebook, Inc., 2008), p.120.

[8] Philip Yancey, "The Day I'll Get My Friends Back," *Christianity Today,* April 3, 1995, p.120.

[9] Henry David Thoreau, quoted in Gail Perry and Jill Perry, eds., *A Rumor of Angels: Quotations for Living, Dying and Letting Go* (New York: MacMillan, 1989), p.54.

[10] Seneca, quoted in Franklin Pierce Adams, ed., *The Book of Quotations* (New York: Frank and Wangels, 1942), p.364.

[11] Robert Buckman, *I Didn't Know What to Say* (New York: Little Brown, 1989), p.11.

[12] John Carmody, *Toward a Male Spirituality* (Mystic, CT: Twenty-Third Publications, 1990), p.92.

[13] Smith, *Grieving the Death of a Friend,* p.119.

[14] Smith, *Friendgrief,* p.217.

[15] Ibid., adapted, p.120.

[16] Ibid., p.70.

[17] Ibid., pp.270-271.

[18] Ibid., p.iv. Used with permission.

Chapter 9: The Loss of a Pet

[1] Wallace Sife, Ph.D., *The Loss of a Pet* (New York: Howell Book House, 2005), p.15.
[2] Alan D. Wolfelt, Ph.D., *When Your Pet Dies* (Ft. Collins, CO: Companion Press, 2004), adapted, pp.11-13.
[3] Moira Anderson Allen, M.Ed., *Coping with Sorrow on the Loss of Your Pet* (Loveland, CO: Alpine, 1996), p.45.
[4] Jan Katz, *Going Home* (New York: Random House, 2012), adapted, p.29.
[5] Ibid., pp.95-96.
[6] Lorri A. Greene, Ph.D. and Jacquelyn Landis, *Saying Good-bye to the Pet You Love* (Oakland, CA: New Harbinger, 2002), p.53.
[7] Sife, *The Loss of a Pet,* p.111.
[8] Allen, *Coping with Sorrow on the Loss of Your Pet,* p.65.
[9] Ibid., p.66.
[10] Sife, *The Loss of a Pet,* adapted, pp.149-151.

[11] Ibid., pp.214-223.
[12] Allen, *Coping with Sorrow on the Loss of Your Pet,* adapted, pp.91-95.
[13] Katz, *Going Home,* p.11.
[14] Ibid., p.62.
[15] Allen, *Coping with Sorrow on the Loss of Your Pet,* p.78.

Chapter 10: The Questions of Life

[1] Lewis Smedes, *How Can It Be All Right When Everything Is All Wrong?* (New York: Harper and Row, 1982), p.3.
[2] Billy Cox, "Wallenda's History: One of the Greatest Tragedies," *The Herald Tribune,* June 12, 2012.
[3] Don Baker, *Pain's Hidden Purpose* (Portland, OR: Multnomah Press, 1984), p.72.
[4] Lloyd John Ogilvie, *Why Not? Accept Christ's Healing and Wholeness* (Old Tappan, NJ: Fleming H. Revell, 1985), p.162.
[5] Cordelia Spitzer, "Here Comes Jesus Walking on Water," 1980.

[6] Larry Richards, *When It Hurts Too Much to Wait* (Dallas, TX: Word, Inc., 1985), pp.67-68.

[7] Dr. Elton Mayo, cited in Steve Ogne and Tim Roehl, *TransforMissional Coaching: Empowering Leaders in a Changing Ministry World* (Nashville, TN: B&H Publishing Group, 2008), p.136.

Chapter 11: Helping Others

[1] Harold Kushner, *Living a Life that Matters* (New York: Anchor Books, 2002), pp.123-124.

[2] Frederick Buechner, *Peculiar Treasures: A Biblical Who's Who* (New York: Harper and Row, 1979), p.65.

[3] Kenneth Iserson, MD, *Grave Words* (Tucson, AZ: Galen Press, LTD, 1999), adapted, pp.49-51.

[4] J. Rupp, *Praying Our Goodbyes* (Notre Dame, IN: Ave Maria Press, 1988), p.79.

[5] Lisa Barnes Lampman, *Helping a Neighbor in Crisis* (Wheaton, IL: Tyndale, 1997), p.68.

Additional Resources

The following organizations can provide you with additional help and support as you go through the process of grieving:

American Association of Suicidology (AAS)
5221 Wisconsin Avenue NW,
 Washington, DC 20015
Phone: (202) 237-2280
Website: www.suicidology.org

AAS can supply information to lead families of suicide victims to local resources, such as survivors' groups. Provides literature about suicide and other help for the bereaved.

The American Childhood Cancer Organization
P.O. Box 498, Kensington, MD
 20895-0498
Phone: (855) 858-2226
Website: www.acco.org

This organization is devoted to supporting parents of children who have had or now have cancer.

Child Find of America, Inc.
P.O. Box 277, New Paltz, NY 12561
Phone: (845) 883-6060 •
1-800-I-AM-LOST
Website: www.childfindofamerica.org

Child Find assists parents in finding their missing children. It also offers counseling services for families of missing children.

The Compassionate Friends (TFC)
P.O. Box 3696, Oak Brook, IL 60522
Phone: (630) 990-0010 • (877) 969-0010
Website: www.compassionatefriends.org

TFC has been a cornerstone for bereaved parents throughout the United States as well as internationally.

Mothers Against Drunk Drivers (MADD)
MADD National Office
511 E. John Carpenter Freeway, Suite 700, Irving, TX 75062
Phone: (877) ASK-MADD
Website: www.madd.org

The mission of Mothers Against Drunk Driving (MADD) is to stop drunk driving, support the victims of violent crime, and prevent underage drinking.

National SIDS/Infant Death Resource Center
2115 Wisconsin Avenue NW, Suite 601, Washington, DC 20007-2292
Phone: (866) 866-7437
Website: www.sidscenter.org

The Clearinghouse offers helpful literature on sudden infant death syndrome (SIDS), including reports on the latest medical research.

National SIDS Alliance/First Candle
1314 Bedford Avenue, Suite 210, Baltimore, MD 21208
Phone: (800) 221-7437
Website: www.info@firstcandle.org

The National SIDS Alliance helps parents deal with the shock and grief of losing a baby to SIDS.

National Organization of Parents of Murdered Children, Inc.
4960 Ridge Ave., Suite #2, Cincinnati, OH 45209
Phone: (513) 721-5683
Website: www.pomc.com

The mission of the National Organization of Parents of Murdered Children is to provide support and assistance to all survivors of homicide victims while working to create a world free of murder.

OTHER TITLES FROM
H. NORMAN WRIGHT

Bringing Out the Best in Your Husband
ISBN 978-0-8307-5578-3

Bringing Out the Best in Your Wife
ISBN 978-0-8307-5579-0

The Complete Guide to Crisis and Trauma Counseling
ISBN 978-0-8307-5840-1

Healing Grace for Hurting People
ISBN 978-0-8307-4395-7

Helping Those in Grief
ISBN 978-0-8307-5871-5

Communication: Key to Your Marriage
ISBN 978-0-8307-4793-1

Available at Bookstores Everywhere!
Go to **www.regalbooks.com** to learn more about your favorite Regal books and authors. Visit us online today!

God's Word for Your World™
www.regalbooks.com

Front Cover Flap

FROM
Grieving the *Loss* of a Loved one:

When grief is your close companion, you experience it in many ways. It permeates and changes your feelings, thoughts and attitudes. Why does everyone have to go through this experience? What is its purpose?

- Through grief, you express your feelings about the loss.
- Through grief, you express your protest at the loss, as well as your desire to change what happened and have it not be true. This is a normal response.
- Through grief, you express the effects you have experienced from the devastating impact of the loss.
- Through grief, you may experience God in a new way that changes your life. As Job said, "My ears had heard of you before, but now my eyes have seen you" (Job 42:5, *NCV*).

403

Find out how the process of grieving can help you heal and bring you strength for a hopeful future.

Back Cover Flap

H. Norman Wright is a grief and trauma therapist and responds to national disasters. He has experienced the personal loss of a son, Matthew, and his wife, Joyce. He is on the faculty of Talbot School of Theology and has authored more than 90 books, including the bestsellers *Always Daddy's Girl, Before You Say I Do,* and *Communication: Key to Your Marriage.* He and his wife, Tess, live in Bakersfield, California.

Back Cover Material

A Guide Through the Valley of Loss

Losing a family member is one of life's most difficult experiences. Whether you are facing the death of a spouse, parent, child, sibling, close friend or pet, the weeks and months that follow such a loss can be overwhelming. *Grieving the Loss of a Loved One* is a trustworthy companion for your journey through grief. With gentle honesty and wisdom, bestselling author and respected family therapist H. Norman Wright shares about the process of mourning, the disruption and reordering of family life, and the conflicting and confusing emotions that follow a death in the family. He also shows how it's possible to grow closer to God and other family members as you face the darkness together. You are not alone through the valley—God's Spirit, the Comforter, walks with you every step of the way and will guide you toward true peace and renewed hope.